cybercon

Scott– I hope this
book and its
important message!!
you enjoy

Published by Mindstir Media, LLC
45 Lafayette Rd | Suite 181| North Hampton, NH 03862 | USA
1.800.767.0531 | www.mindstirmedia.com

Printed in the United States of America
ISBN-13: 978-1-7342210-9-1
Library of Congress Control Number: 2019918962

cybercon

PROTECTING OURSELVES FROM BIG TECH & BIGGER LIES

JAMES L. NORRIE

ENDORSEMENTS

"Excellence in People, Process and Technology have always been the keys to a successful organization. However, when it comes to cyber-threat management, the emphasis by most has been on process and technology, not people...with increasingly disastrous results. In his latest book, Dr. Norrie identifies underlying reasons for the "people risk gap", providing a structure and framework to enable a more effective cybersecurity strategy for the human risks present in all organizations."

—Craigg Ballance
Retired Bank Executive & Director,
Canadian Member Services FS-ISAC

"Do parasailing and cybersecurity intersect? Learn how when you read this book! Fascinating. A heartfelt ground-breaker that convincingly transforms cybersecurity conversations from fear to hope..."

—Carol-Ann Hamilton
Best-selling author, consultant, speaker,
and national radio show host

"In business today, we have done everything we can to secure technology and still there are breaches. The missing component is the human element of cybersecurity which this author explores in a compelling and convincing way that will help us all stay safer online. Well done!"

—Mark Ripplinger, President & CEO, Everlink Payment Services

"Cybersecurity keeps executives up at night, wondering if they will be the next headline-making victim of an unfortunate cyberattack that hurts their customers and harms their brand. Given we are all just one click away from scandal, I recommend this book to any leader of any organization…it provides a blueprint for mitigating the human side of cybersecurity, something most organizations are simply missing."

—Barry Clavir, Founder and CEO, Leader's Beyond Inc.

"Buy it. Read it. Do it. Genius!"

—Tracy Abbott, Chief Compliance Officer

"As someone who does not truly understand the intricacies of the world of technology, I found this book very revealing. It gives voice to many of my own fears, and offers hope for the future. It is inspired reading for anyone concerned about society's collective online destiny."

—Dr. Judith A. Kirkpatrick, retired Professor, Dean and Provost

"Once again, Dr Norrie cuts straight to the root cause of contemporary online hacks with a refreshing change from the usual fear-mongering to an innovative approach that encourages education and cooperation."

—Stuart Grant, Chief Compliance Officer

"If you want to fight hackers, change tactics. Cyberattacks are more prevalent than ever, touching work and families all the time. Big Tech & Bigger Lies can help you SAVE yourself from yourself and protect your money in an age of increasing cyber vulnerability. Upgrade your online behavior today!"

—Kyle Reid and Cheryl Purves, Small Business Owners

"As a cybersecurity professional who consults about keeping organizations safe, I am always striving to learn about the latest advances in our field. Time and again we blame cyber breaches on the technology, which fails to recognize the human element that is ultimately the most important factor. This book solves that puzzle!"

—Ajay Randhawa, Cybersecurity Consultant

"Are you at risk? Or maybe your family or workplace? This book addresses our human vulnerabilities online, and Dr. Norrie offers innovative strategies to combat these issues helping make surfing safer for us all."

—Harley Ranson, Retired Aviation Engineering Executive

DEDICATION

To all the cybersecurity professionals and academic colleagues I know who really get it, working to keep us all safer online. To my patron, Chloe Eichelberger, whose generosity, inspired intellect, and spirited debate nurtured my early thoughts on this subject. To my patient and loving partner who is my biggest fan! To my family, and especially my Mom and daughters—sometimes far away but never far from my heart - and dear friends, who when I promised to never write another book, supported me in this adventure anyway. I love you all for so many wonderful reasons, but all the more for this kind indulgence!

TABLE OF CONTENTS

PROLOGUE

We all have an online history, and mine is directly related to this book. As the owner of a business that depends on the internet, I can recount first-hand just how important cybersecurity is. But there is more to my story that is directly relevant, so let me begin by going back to the fall of 2016. I received a call from our IT manager. The panic in his voice was palpable...

Customer traffic to our website had been geometrically increasing for almost two years because of our razer-sharp focus on rolling out a robust global digital footprint. This took considerable energy and resources. But with online success came the unavoidable security issues we always anticipated, and thought we had thoroughly prepared for. But that phone call turned that naive assumption on its head as we experienced our *first* fully blown digital nightmare.

Our website had been successfully hacked. It came crashing down right in the middle of the critical holiday shopping season – something my business really depended on. No new leads, lost holiday sales, and no interface for our customers. In pre-internet terms, our beautifully designed store on 5th avenue, enticing huge numbers of passersby's to come in and browse, became instantly invisible and the front doors locked. No storefront. No window display. No signage. Everything was gone. It was scary.

After the mad scramble to recover, I obsessed with a multitude of questions. Why us? Who would do this? We're not a big bank or a public company. Was this some random Australian high school student with too much time on his or her hands since that is where the attack had started? Or was our traffic being hijacked to a "money site"? Maybe this was the devious work of a jealous and malicious competitor? Or an attempt to mine our large database of sensitive customer information?

In the end, it turned out to be the latter - this time by Russian and Ukrainian automated bots mining our site for rich data which, fortunately for us, wasn't linked in any way to our website. We were lucky.

My after-the-fact response to this incident is what any business owner would do. I demanded the implementation of a host of expensive Fortune 50 level security protections. Although I knew this wouldn't make us bulletproof (no one really is), at least we would become *significantly* less vulnerable, maybe able to sleep a bit more soundly at night knowing we had done everything we could.

Or at least I thought so. Until that fateful fall day of 2019. I had just gotten back from the gym and pulled out my cell phone to check my email. A new message had just been sent from one of my most trusted senior staff. It read:

> Subject - Wire Transfer Confirmation
> Hi Alan,
>
> Here is the wire transfer confirmation.
> They should have the funds tomorrow.

I was horrified and called immediately asking - WHAT TRANSFER??? The confident, almost indignant "what do you mean what transfer!' voice explained details of the $43,000USD transfer to another country that had been processed per my instructions in a series of emails exchanged between us throughout the day. Of course, predictably, the problem was I had not sent any of those e-mails.

Then came silence. My employee had been carefully and artfully spear-fished using a spoofed e-mail address that was hauntingly close to my real e-mail ID. It was an easy mistake, a human error. But this loyal employee now realized she had been duped.

There followed a horrified "OH MY GOD ALAN" followed by a gasp filled with excruciating terror and embarrassment. What to do next?

Again, luck was on our side. The transfer had only just been authorized with our FX partner, and not yet forwarded into the foreign bank account. So we were able to quickly recall it. But a mere matter of minutes later and the ending to this story would have been entirely different. And the outcome would have generated a substantial and unrecoverable business loss for which there was no recourse.

This was my second cyber unawareness epiphany. It unfolded just exactly as described inside this very book. Today it's not enough, not ever going to be enough, to protect your IT assets with the very latest and most sophisticated cybersecurity technology. That alone cannot keep us safe, although that effort has value. Instead, I learned my own lesson the hard way. The next wave of digital warfare will certainly be waged with computers and technology, but not targeting us directly from outside the organization, but rather indirectly using our most precious assets - human beings – against us from the inside.

Dr. Norrie has understood this, and has been teaching this new reality of human hacks to business leaders for many years, passionately beating the warning drum that no amount of time or money spent on technology tools, punitive threats, or even generic awareness training about these new threats will ultimately *change behavior*. Our biggest cyber threats will now come in the form of sophisticated and pernicious attacks that target basic human vulnerabilities. And he has produced a powerful and *holistic* system that comprehends that reality with practical solutions that actually work, aligned to each of our individual personality traits and online instincts. He takes this fight personally and it shows.

On hearing my tale of cyber woe, my friend shared his manuscript, test and training plans with me in its early days. In fact, he eventually shared them with my whole company. And it worked. I was the very first organization to pilot his then evolving system, and it could not have been more timely or valuable. I read his book in wonder at the timing of his writing effort and my recent breach: with each new page, it gave voice to my worst fears, but also provided hope and positive solutions that we might all eventually prevail and make ourselves safer online. I felt better just for having read it.

I have now seen these transformative tools at work. When my employees understand what types of online threats they are most vulnerable to, and are given the tools to check and double check methods to mitigate those threats, we are all more secure as a result. We have created a culture of "we're all in this together". And what company couldn't use an increased dose of that?

While mine is only one story, and personal to the author and me, I also think its representative of what is really happening in the world. ANY business – or individual or family for that matter – is at risk of being exploited online. That threat is growing and so is our fear.

As the author so eloquently notes, our growing use of technology only makes us more vulnerable. Throwing more technology at this problem will not solve it. Yet, we also cannot also live in a state of constant fear or complacency either. Instead, only each of us can solve this dilemma by empowering ourselves with new knowledge and new approaches. This book does that. I urge you to read it and internalize its message. Then take the test and start to figure out how you can keep yourself, your family and your organization safer online, because that benefits everyone, everywhere.

—Alan Merriam, CEO
Merriam Music
Toronto, Ontario

INTRODUCTION:
THE WRONG APPROACH TO THE PROBLEM

Cybersecurity is **not** primarily a technology issue. It is a human behavior problem on a massively networked scale. Denial of this fact, driven by the drumbeat of Big Tech profits and false promises, is not productive, does not keep us safe online, and works to society's detriment. This book explores how and why this is happening and what you can do about it. It is about empowerment rather than victimhood, sweeping away online fear and replacing it with hope.

When humans perceive danger, a natural physiological *fight-or-flight* response is triggered. Fears about online cybersecurity risks provoke this autonomic stress response, and it is not under our control. Rather, this instinct developed as an evolutionary response over centuries for the self-preservation of our species. That means every single one of us is somehow affected whenever we enter this state, whether or not we recognize and accept it.

Hyperarousal, once triggered, instantly washes our bodies in bio-chemicals that heighten our senses. These bio-chemicals include cortisol to enhance blood sugar, increase our blood pressure, and suppress the immune system to temporarily increase energy. Testosterone to boost strength; dopamine and serotonin to enhance brain function and suppress our normal pain response; and adrenaline to support the immediate physical response of either fight or flight. These hormones are powerful chemicals: if they were pharmaceuticals, they would surely be controlled substances requiring a prescription!

Of fundamental importance to this book is the notion that hyper-arousal, and its associated condition of hypervigilance (an enhanced state of sensory sensitivity accompanied by an exaggerated intensity of behaviors whose purpose is to detect dangerous activity), trigger a state of increased anxiety-causing *complacency and exhaustion*. As we become complacent and exhausted, we make increasingly worse decisions about dangerous situations. This can result in an endless loop of stress and anxiety, including and perhaps especially when we are online.

By nature, this mental state must be *temporary* because our bodies cannot sustain this condition for prolonged periods because of its negative biological consequences. Research has shown that if this state is perpetually triggered, eventually we become less and less able to withstand it, becoming *desperate* to return our bodies to a normal state by eliminating, escaping, or ignoring our fear. In extreme cases, it can cause a yearning for death, a highly dangerous state of mind with its own set of attendant consequences leading to higher rates of mental illness and suicide. Sound familiar? Two decades of statistics now prove an increasing trend for both of these outcomes around the world, without a satisfactory explanation yet.

But I suspect a strong connection to our growing online social behavior because we are truly engaged in a grand human experiment. Yet, in this current period of technology development, the long-term consequences of this experiment remain a mystery as we proactively disintermediate human physical and social connection and replace it with technology substitutes. This cannot help but subtly affect human evolution over time. As a species, we are always adapting our underlying human condition to match our environment to improve survival. This will be no different of course.

As with any longitudinal social change, the human impact and societal consequences of this shift will take decades to emerge. But they will. And while social science research methodology makes it hard to claim a measurable cause and effect relationship among these changes, it seems intuitively obvious that as technology-induced fear increases, so does widespread generalized social anxiety. How that impacts society will depend on how we all adapt our social responses over time.

As part of the human condition, we do not relish being afraid. We rather seek to avoid it. But today, this fear is autonomously triggered by simply living in a tech-laden social environment that virtually demands participation. Whether we like it or not, simply by being aware, we gain knowledge of new technologies and their inherent risks. We then delve into this technically enabled artificial world embedding these lurking fears ever deeper into our psyche.

This makes it possible for the plague of cybercrime, political manipulation, information overload, and online anxiety that pervades the internet today to trigger hypervigilance in most of us. Big Tech contributes to this fearful state of mind by offering an array of ever-expanding social media platforms and similar technologies, unregulated and unrestricted, to create a globally interconnected, but also potentially more dangerous, world.

In response, many cybersecurity professionals in the workplace, who I know care deeply about protecting the information assets of their organizations, give in to this fear, perhaps embracing and supporting it as a way to enhance individual awareness of cybersecurity risks. This translates to an outcome—*whether we are at home or at work*—where we feel perpetually, perhaps subconsciously, afraid of technology. And this is dangerous because it exhausts us.

More of us than ever live in some state of this sustained fear, whether or not we participate in online activities and platforms. As peer pressure to be present online grows, users begin to depend on these systems for a variety of new online social activities and outlets, perhaps even believing they *need* them to be socially connected. Researchers refer to this as technology-intermediated social transactions—and they function differently than those we seek and maintain in person. This means just going online triggers broad personal, professional and social impacts.

As we examine this topic together, I will explore how this impacts our mental health, emotional stability, and psychological conditioning. I can prove technology changes our behavior at work, and that has implications for an organization's cybersecurity efforts. Later, I will also link this state of fear to increasing rates of depression, suicide, domestic terrorism, religious radicalization, and global political interference on a grand scale. I will present how it haunts our elderly who are especially vulnerable because of technical naiveté, leading to cruel hacks and attacks which leave them feeling more alone, socially embarrassed, and broke. And we will explore the ever-present online dangers for our youth, who may not have sufficient developmental experience to properly understand and manage their online behavior.

Regardless of the cause, this constant state of fear underpins many important social consequences that are interconnected in cause and effect creating impact on every single one of us, both personally and professionally. Technology progress is now erasing hope in vast tracks of society as we simply become resigned to being afraid, manipulated and deceived online.

So while selling the value of their new digital inventions to investors and consumers, Big Tech denies responsibility for these consequences. And they actively deflect efforts by government regulators to bring them to account too. They depend on our unbridled sharing of personal information of all sorts, both appropriate and inappropriate, and actively attack anyone who criticizes them—including me—as Luddites who must not understand the democracy-building characteristics of new social technologies that rise above tyranny and censorship to invite self-expression. But that argument is ultimately self-serving. And false.

Of course, there are kernels of truth in the defense that not all technology is bad. It can deliver on some of its promise and potential. But Big Tech generally overpromises and under-delivers, and therein lies an important truth: the introduction of all this technology is what creates cybersecurity risk in the first place. Cybersecurity exists as a massive and costly worldwide problem simply because online technology exists on a similarly massive scale.

So how do these self-proclaimed "technology breakthroughs" really benefit society versus enriching the companies that produce and promote these leaky platforms? We know from public disclosures that these companies are benefitting economically at unprecedented rates from our "free" use of their platforms. But what proof do they proffer of positive impacts to offset the abundant proof of the negative impacts these technologies are imposing on civil societies around the globe? This gap represents a real human cost of incalculable proportions.

Why? Because complete online cybersecurity is *never* possible. It is a myth. All systems are vulnerable—it is only a question of degree. So long as systems are ultimately designed, operated, and inhabited online by humans who are frail and vulnerable, there will be mistakes. Therefore, simply being online brings some level of inherent risk to each of us because we make mistakes. All we can do is mitigate these growing risks through sensible participation and awareness. And most of us already do that in our offline lives anyway: we balance overall risk and reward and are self-managed when and how we choose to engage in risky behavior.

Technology companies, and any company that operates online actually, possess personal information about us that others would like to steal and exploit. To keep us confident in sharing this information with them, they make us believe the answer to increasing overall cybersecurity lies in enhancing technology to make computer networks safer. But they know there is no guarantee, so they hint at their innate ability to keep us safe online, trying to overcome our fear of participation. But what they are really doing is protecting their ability to grow their own profits. That goal will always come first, driving another important conclusion of this book—commercial self-interest drives corporate behavior and decision-making.

Some consumers may prefer to deny this obvious conclusion. They continue to participate in Big Tech's artificially crafted online worlds, enjoying what benefits that may bring, but always assuming they should be able to hold someone else accountable for keeping them safe online. If they ask us to share personal information, surely these companies know how to keep it safe, right? But that is a misplaced vote of confidence in Big Tech. More sophisticated companies may know more about how to keep your personal information safe, how to ensure that systematic backups prevent risk, and how to build redundant systems to increase service levels. But not all companies either know how to or can apparently afford to do so. That is why these attacks succeed, and why they are never going away because there will always be frailties and vulnerabilities as technology and humans intersect and interact.

The truth of the matter is, technologists have done everything they likely can to this point in purely technical terms, yet it has not kept online participants safe. So we are all just only one click away from disaster most of the time. I conclude that the biggest risk involving technology is not the technology itself, but human use and abuse of it. Therefore the dominant cybersecurity issue is not *technical* hacks but *human* hacks.

How Am I Most Personally Vulnerable?

Technology-based cybersecurity efforts today, no matter how intense or sophisticated, cannot protect us from *self-inflicted harm*. Systems engage innate human behavior—both good and bad—and unlike technology, the human condition is complex, immutable over centuries of evolution, and is not easily predicted, interdicted, or controlled.

This obvious frailty—because humans are flawed—is the truth that makes our fear about these platforms so valid. Social media especially are susceptible to exploitation simply because they assemble humans, who are unpredictable and can be dangerous, into a technically intermediated and largely unregulated online ecosystem. Mistakes will happen, and harm will occur by definition. As we experience or hear about more and more unfortunate incidents online, the associated negative impact of learning about this makes us more and more afraid. This naturally triggers our fight-or-flight response. And the cycle begins and repeats.

Yet the state of hyperarousal/hypervigilance that online technologies trigger in humans is ultimately counterproductive. To overcome it, we must become empowered to understand and manage the risks these social media platforms *individually* represent, and those are *quite personal to each of us*. To accomplish that, we must learn more about ourselves, becoming self-aware of the risks we inherently undertake when we go online, learning to mitigate and manage them for our own benefit. We can't rely on a company, more interested in profits than people, to do this for us. And that is the *"cybercon"* referred to in the title of this book that Big Tech wants us all to buy into. But it won't succeed because society is beginning to figure out these essential Big Tech lies and broken promises, rapidly calling them out for what they are.

It is self-deceiving to think anybody but you can save you from your online instincts. While government regulation, potential new laws, and questioning Big Tech motives are important issues to explore in this book, the personal value of *cyber self-regulation* cannot be reinforced enough for the benefits they bring to you, your family, and to organizations.

So this book can help everyone become more cyberaware. It proposes self-directed safer online practices aligned to your instincts and habits. It demands you get engaged in global cybersecurity issues that are rapidly arising in novel ways. These can have potential personal impacts you must be aware of, not afraid of. And I conclude that mastery of *technology-induced fear* is ultimately the surest path to curbing recurring, risky online behaviors successfully. Acquiring new knowledge and perspectives can help each of us overcome fear by taking appropriate actions to reduce personal risk. We become part of the solution, not the problem.

Ultimately, this is the most significant Big Tech lie: while they <u>can</u> help us *stay safer online* technically, they cannot make us personally *behave more safely online*. Cybersecurity is ultimately a personal pursuit, and Big Tech knows it. It is up to each of us alone to achieve.

In mastering these nuances of behaving safely online, I intend this book to help you feel less afraid, more in control, and ultimately more effective at cybersecurity than you ever thought humanly possible. I want internet participation to be safe, fun, and productive for all. I want to protect and preserve technology innovations for the greater social good instead of greater evil. To accomplish this requires we all transform user fear into hope, making cybersecurity a very personal social and human mission globally.

CHAPTER ONE:
CYBER AS A STATE OF MIND

Technological progress is inevitable, and as Moore's Law defines, relentlessly exponential. Especially in the recent course of human history, society has experienced the rapid ascent of technology. But is that pace of technology change now outstripping society's ability to adapt? Human evolution takes time, and we are on the cusp of a startling Fourth Industrial Revolution that will not treat all of society equally well[1]. As a result, technology progress will turn into social disruption, and trigger unforeseen and unintended consequences. In fact, some inventors report deep regret as the true risks of the technology they created later emerge, and as widespread adoption imposes unintended consequences on all humanity. But ignorance of this only breeds fear. Instead, we need to explore it and use new knowledge to inspire hope.

We sit at a critical inflection point in terms of current cycles of tech innovation and disruption as it relates to social media platforms. Facebook—the mother of all social media platforms literally—was only

---

1   See the informative video from the World Economic Forum: *What is the Fourth Industrial Revolution?*

founded in February 2004. That makes it less than twenty years old as a technology; but, frankly, it seems like it's been around forever, doesn't it? And that is part of what technology progress does. It culturally envelops us, and before we know it, we embrace it without due regard to the potential good and bad that adoptive impulse creates. This is particularly true when the technology has no cost and spreads virtually and virally as Facebook and others have done globally. Before we know it, they **are** the de facto status quo and they exert powerful social, political and economic influence as a result.

However, we should be mindful that online social behaviors are simply adaptations of how humans have always behaved. They are not really new. For instance, where we had crimes like theft, fraud, and impersonation before Facebook, we have them on Facebook today. And we will have them after Facebook when that time comes when Facebook too fades into human history. That is because these systems simply *transfer* existing human behaviors into *new online forms*. For example, social engineering is simply basic fraud—one of the oldest tricks in the human history book—but masking in new online disguises. This demonstrates social media technology as enabling human potential for both good and bad, mirroring our innate human nature. This also suggests not becoming over-wrought with fear about all this – its just a normal part of human nature that has been with us for centuries actually.

Of course, Big Tech only promotes the positive potential of their latest inventions, often denying obvious negative social impacts, even when they are obviously visible. That is what good marketing does: it accentuates the positive promise of any new product. Further, everyone really wants to secretly believe the marketing hype and assume new technology must be good technology. To do otherwise risks being labeled anti-technology—someone who simply "doesn't get it." But perhaps you *do* get it, harboring a deep-down niggling sense this isn't just quite right and that it could lead to bad outcomes. You are slowly entering a state of hypervigilance.

Over time, constant media coverage of the cybersecurity risks of new technology confirm your looming fear that there are online dangers. Stories spread and evidence mounts of these platforms enabling cyber bullying, real-time online group suicides, boastful sharing of criminal activity as a badge of honor, and recruiting of domestic terrorists to inflict mass shootings on innocents. Reports show the multitude of illicit ways criminals prey on our innocent children, teenagers, and our elderly particularly, exploiting their sense of trust in these social platforms for criminal gain, inflicting great personal harm to many.

In this environment, our initial giddy sense of progress is replaced with dread: what has been created and why did they do that? A sense of retrospective loss replaces the anticipation of the joy of progress as new tools are used in new ways to perpetuate old deeds, continually proving the darker side of humanity. But the human condition itself has not changed—only the speed and scope of the online platforms available to demonstrate its evil side has.

Contemporary culture and mass media often treat all of this as new. It is not. These human behaviors have always been present and were always a risk. Moving online, they just present more often because of the ease of reaching billions of people worldwide in a single click from any place in the world now. And that scale is the only really new part to this story.

The thing that has really changed is speed and how easy these negative exploits are to accomplish, reducing the friction required for humans to engage in hurtful, demeaning, or criminal acts globally by targeting millions of us all at once. This is the "progress" we have been pursuing in creating a completely technology-enabled and interconnected planet.

Of course, claims of the good these platforms engender are fair. Some aspects of new technology can expand human horizons and create positive changes. But as with most things throughout history, the speed of evil adoption seems always to outpace the good, and negative news is more swiftly shared than good news. This contributes to our gnawing fear. So, we tilt away from anticipation of the good to an overwhelming sense of dread about the bad. But if we only worry about risks, we never end up having any fun—and that's sad.

So, we have to understand this instinct as opposed to simply giving into it. We know it can provoke a continuous sense of hypervigilance, risking escalation to hyperarousal, inviting the natural fight-or-flight response that is so much a part of our human condition. Remaining locked in cycles of detecting and responding to fear and danger is not sustainable; so, we seek ways to resolve this state even if they are not always helpful. The options can include withdrawal from participation in what we perceive as a dangerous activity; attempting to mitigate or reduce the fear of harm or perceived dangers; imposing controls of constraints to make ourselves feel better when we do undertake the activity; or simply ignoring the harm and potential danger and engaging in the behavior anyway, accepting whatever consequences that brings.

I want to pause for a moment. It is this last option—avoidance—that creates the most dangerous online cybersecurity outcome for most people and what I worry most about from my research. *It means we participate fully while suppressing signs of danger ahead.*

In presentations, I refer to this as a **cyber state of mind**: *blissful participation tinged with willful ignorance.* This is an obviously dangerous state of mind that increases our online risk and leads us astray. But being in a more aware state constantly triggers uncomfortable biological reactions we yearn to avoid. So, through denial, we enter this cyber state of mind to reduce our inherent sense of looming danger. Yet, as this cycle becomes self-perpetuating over time, managing these feelings is at the very core of enhancing our personal cybersecurity.

In a repressed state of denial, we engage with technology feeling almost normal, deliberately dinting any looming sense of danger. We continue online behaviors without grasping fully the real risks they represent, moving into an almost trance-like state of using something for whatever purposes we feel are urgent and important enough to tempt us into participation while ignoring danger. We have been lulled into complacency.

This means we lose sight of how to keep ourselves safe, especially where simple modifications to our online behaviors might mitigate risk and legitimately make us feel less afraid. Ironically, being afraid now drives us to *cyber ignorance* making us more vulnerable to the very things of which we are now afraid. That is substantively ironic to me.

What should we do? To properly secure the relief from hypervigilance we biologically crave, we must become more self-aware of our particular technology-induced behaviors and when they promote or demote our online safety. We must learn how our personal online behavior makes us more or less vulnerable and why each of us potentially exhibits a unique set of online risks. For ease of reference, I adopt the term "cyberaware" throughout—a state of being more reflective about how more informed use of new technologies can help us feel less afraid. Essentially this means acquiring new knowledge about our existing online instincts.

By accomplishing this, we begin to disassemble and then reconstruct our own online behavior. We are enabled to compare the risks and rewards of how we are behaving instead of blindly adopting new technology just because. We can *choose* how we are going to adopt, or not, various technology innovations for our own future benefit instead of Big Tech's.

By rejecting wholesale adoption of new technologies across society until we resolve cognitive concerns about their implications in advance, we all become more personally empowered to modify our online behavior in response to technology changes over time. *This maximizes our personal gain while minimizing our risk.* Notably, this is also exactly how humans approach this problem in the offline world.

Witness, for example, being on vacation and seeing others parasailing over the warm waters of the Caribbean. They appear to be having lots of fun. You do not see any obvious evidence of danger after watching them from your perch under a beach umbrella. Because you have never done this before, you are naturally *cautious*, but not necessarily afraid. At this point you arrive at an inflection point: you might, for instance, decide to look online for statistics about how safe parasailing is. You discover negative coverage indicating just how dangerous this activity is. As you research further, you discover stories and videos showing actual injuries or fatalities from this activity. Your mind begins to race. Remember, you haven't decided yet IF you are going to do this particular activity; rather, you are investigating the risks and rewards of that potential decision. Depending on your risk tolerance, you may dismiss parasailing as an option, and returned to the safer realm of reading a book on the beach. Or, if you are more risk-tolerant or torn, you may still be in a state of cautious consideration.

Continuing, you venture closer to a final decision and walk toward the kiosk where the activity is booked and paid for. You speak to the attendants and learn more about both the rewards (fun, fun, fun!) and the risks. They explain what they do to ensure your safety, perhaps handing you a list of safety and security features they claim (training, life jacket, experienced personnel, specially designed non-tangling harness, etc.). Of course, they leave until the end the legal waiver you will eventually have to sign ensuring that you are responsible for the decision you are about to make, accepting no liability for any personal injury or death!

This description, even if you have never parasailed on a beach, should be reminiscent of how you actually approach a decision to engage in any new activity. You compare the risks and rewards and self-determine your level of comfort. If the activity seems too dangerous, your flight response will kick in, and you will abandon any idea of participating, perhaps literally running in the opposite direction! Or, if the activity seems to offer more potential for benefit and fun under the sun, and you perceive the risk as manageable, you shake off the fear and sign up.

Whatever your decision, it is an inherently *personal one* over which you have complete control. It should not be about following the crowd because that requires giving into peer pressure, also not good, and more likely as a provoking factor in our behavior as kids or teenagers. Instead, as adults, we must adjudicate this decision on its own merits, and on a risk-adjusted basis. We each use our own intuition after securing facts about how this decision may impact us either way.

Seemingly we abandon these important checks and balances when it comes to our instincts about new technology, apps, or social media platforms. As others adopt it in a frenzy of enthusiasm—online invitations to participate overflowing your inbox and peer pressure to post increasing—you feel left out unless you immediately accept and engage. You repost, share, and invite others wantonly pushing ever more of your personal life online. That is peer pressure.

Left aside is taking time to determine for yourself how you may or may not benefit from that online participation, and social judgment being what it is, you may sense negative social consequences will arise, secretly fearing rejection if you elect to sit it out. So, you dive right in and initially, our participation seems innocent, fun, and maybe even interesting. However, in the back of your uncontrollable mind is a sense of dread about what you are doing. Might it be dangerous and pose unknown risks? You may even learn something you innocently did online is now reported as being a risky behavior, making the fear conscious[2]. All this cumulatively intrudes into our psyche triggering that ever-recurring fight-or-flight response.

What now? Well, you continue to participate because you have already decided to do so—but your brain is crying out for you to reassess and rethink your decision. Maybe it's not safe! So, the biological trap becomes obvious: this is not a sustainable state for very long because we do not like feeling afraid, and something has to give to reduce these feelings of anxiety.

As I stressed earlier, a first step is to properly evaluate risks and to take the time to do so *before* participating. That definitely helps. However, often with new inventions or applications, we have neither the time to do so or access to the information about the real risks and results of participating, before we feel drawn into this peer-driven web of participation.

---

2   See for example: https://www.vox.com/the-goods/2019/7/17/20698271/faceapp-privacy-panic-russia-old-face-filter-app

RISK

REWARD ▶

One thing most of us have is a natural instinct toward assessment of risk and reward that underpins how we react in various situations. We are all either risk seeking, risk neutral or risk averse to some degree. Come to discover, this is an inherent part of our trait-based personality. So, your own inclinations on this are easily detected and examined if you take the time to do so, particularly made easier if you are prompted for what to look for.

For anyone who has been through psychotherapy, this process of uncovering, examining and then repurposing our innate, instinctive responses is a first step in changing them for the better. Or trying to anyway. But most of us need a stimulus to provoke this journey of self-discovery before it can occur. Maybe this book can serve that purpose for your online behavior.

Given our inherent personal calculus as it regards risk and reward, once we understand this, we can potentially adjust our online behavior accordingly to stay within either self-defined safety limits or limits your workplace might establish, for instance. This helps you feel less vulnerable leading to less perceived danger, thereby reducing fear and enhancing your online experiences. Similarly, as we collectively all achieve this state, we begin to experience more positive rather than negative outcomes from our technology participation, enhancing our sense of calmer acceptance of our own technology decisions.

What can be concluded from all this? Big Tech should *not* be allowed to dictate our social participation in their inventions. That should be a personal decision for each of us, exercised thoughtfully and with a complete understanding of the inherent risks and rewards. Peer pressure arising from the rate of adoption of any particular new technology should not be a factor in your personal adoption decision, because not all new technology is good technology. Or, a technology that is good for one person may not be good for another. We must learn to choose.

Reserving these as strictly personal decisions prevents drift into complacency. Otherwise, a self-depleting *negative cyber state of mind* is triggered by forced acceptance of technological progress, participating whether we like it or not. The goal of this book and the test it describes is to help you gain knowledge that empowers you to be safer online, triggering hope and displacing fear so you make better technology decisions in keeping with your instincts. In so doing, we all become less of a risk to ourselves and to others, making online activities safer.

CHAPTER TWO:
THE TEST

For as long as humans have existed, they have exhibited their own individual personalities. As diverse as the DNA that creates our physical characteristics, the make-up of our personalities is a blend of nature and nurture in a constellation of traits in combination that create the dimensions that make each of us unique. Personality defines our personhood.

Of the many ways of examining all that, the psychology I prefer is trait-based personality theory. Most psychologists and sociologists agree that trait-based theories have face validity. This approach can help us better understand ourselves. When properly applied, this theory can describe and explain personality similarities and differences in understandable ways, although there are limitations to this approach just because of the sheer diversity of minute differences in personality humans present.

Nonetheless, it is superior to most other theories such as Freud's psychoanalytic or humanistic approaches and, generally, more accessible to people because they recognize the language in trait-based theory as easily self-applied. And who hasn't taken a personality test at some point in their lives and been amazed at the results? Moreover, if you picked up this book, your natural interest in this subject may have had you do many of these for many different reasons over time just because there are so many behavioral assessment tests.

Thus, it became intriguing to me as a researcher to think about how trait-based personality theory might explain our online behaviors—our cybersecurity profile, as it were. Was it possible that how we behave online and the risks that we run are more aligned to underlying personality traits rather than simply being random? To what extent is our behavior a question of nature—less changeable—versus nurture and experience—and therefore more changeable?

This journey of discovery led to study just about every trait-based personality theory and the many associated behavioral assessments derived from them starting around 1952 until about 1980. At this point, the field became both saturated to some extent; but also quite stable as a well-accepted and validated theory within psychology. Simultaneously, as a society we became quite intrigued by testing, particularly standardized testing, as a way to sort ourselves out.

This research path led me to discover and establish a new approach to detecting, predicting, and interdicting dangerous online behavior, both individually and collectively through standardized testing. At the outset, personality theory was too diverse and had too many traits to easily correlate them to our online behavior—it needed to be simpler to be effective as a predictive tool. This led to an exploration of which specific personality traits most likely affect your actual online behavior. Two very relevant personality traits emerged that consistently show up in how we behave online: the degree to which we are either *risk-tolerant or risk-averse* and an attendant desire and willingness to generally be either a *rule breaker or rule follower*. I wondered: could these two dimensions be reliably assessed and discriminated individually?

If these two specific traits could be detected and predicted successfully, it would help particularly explain why some individuals are more or less prone to third-party inspired exploitations where they respond to or click on something online when they should not, or are somehow induced to share something online when they should know better. Wow!

These two particular axes began to form the basis of my evolving theory on how to profile the cybersecurity risk of any individual, specifically in an on-the-job context. This is increasingly urgent and important in a globally interconnected business world full of online cyber risks, and where so many people and companies daily report being hacked or attacked.

Using a subset of educational testing theory, I was able to eventually isolate and evolve a series of non-invasive test questions that, when ranked by respondents on a Likert scale between 1 and 6, were seemingly predictive of their underlying inherent approach to risk-taking and rule-following behaviors. Through pilot testing, eventually responses to their items were reliably linked to specific traits and were translated to what is essentially a snapshot of an individual's online risk. This breakthrough has since been patented, now proving to be reliable about 93.7% of the time as individuals report a high degree of self-agreement with the test results.

As with any instrument, in about 4.3% of cases, the standardized test can only successfully detect the dominance of one of the two traits and is less equivocal on the other, forcing the respondent to self-identify the more applicable profile. And, the test fails to discriminate less than 2% of the time because the individual exhibits a central mean tendency that makes their presentation of differences so slight the test cannot detect them successfully. That does not mean they do not exist, only that they are intensely moderated. The automated testing method can even detect a respondent who is deliberately trying to provide a pattern of responses instead of being truthful through item intra-correlation. So the test works!

The results of my **CyberIQtest** then deliver a personal cybersecurity profile that locates you in one of four quadrants that I chose to label for easy reference to each specific style:

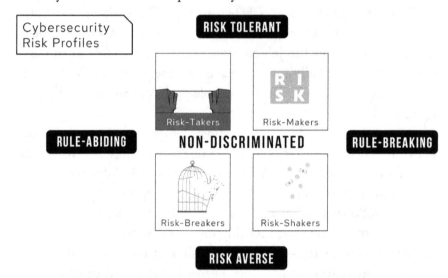

From the illustration you can see that an individual's profile is derived from the extent to which they are either risk tolerant or risk averse on the one hand and rule-abiding or rule-breaking on the other. The test measures your instincts on these dimensions to locate your base personality in one of the four quadrants, or as non-discriminated if you are too in-between.

Further, within each of these quadrants, the test can further detect the strength of expression of the traits associated with that quadrant, resulting in either a moderate or stronger expression within the quadrant—that is, pushing outwards toward the furthest boundary of the behaviors. The labels I chose are tied to the nature of each quadrant to provide a conceptual framework for understanding our innate cybersecurity risks. But I must be entirely clear on an essential point: while each represents a relatively higher or lower risk of being prone to certain types of online exploitation, *anyone* in *any* of these quadrants can be hacked.

The more relevant question is to what degree is someone in a particular quadrant likely to fall prey to what specific types of online hacks and attacks? Also, no one style is *better* or eve *superior* at avoiding attacks, just less vulnerable to some particular kinds of attacks. Or more likely to be more easily trained to avoid their most likely vulnerabilities for example. And they disperse across the quadrants in different ratios in different industries and businesses I have found. So this means there is no "better" test result to have, one over another.

That is because *all* organizations need employees that exhibit *all* four traits because these inherent personality traits apply to many other dimensions of on-the-job behavior besides simply adhering to risk-reducing practices. Therefore, the test is **not** about eliminating a specific kind of person from the organization in order to reduce or control the risk of a cybersecurity incident. Rather, the test can identify specific types of cybersecurity attacks (known as threat vectors) that are *more likely to succeed and why* given any particular individual's particular risk/rule profile. These also creates the opportunity to consider overall rates of risk prevalence and preponderance to risk for the entire organization by mapping its organizational make-up according to the range of people found in each quadrant:

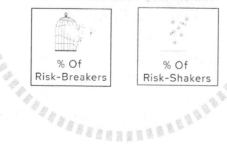

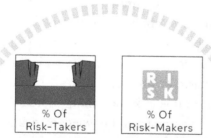

% Of Risk-Takers	% Of Risk-Makers
TOTAL ORGANIZATIONAL RISK	
% Of Risk-Breakers	% Of Risk-Shakers

This can provide those tasked with managing risk and compliance in an organization (or your extended family, church, or club too for that matter) the opportunity to refine optimal mitigation and interdiction strategies across the whole organization by implementing "style-aligned" training and controls for example. So this book and the test are a compliment and adjunct to other cybersecurity efforts already being undertaken. Why is this important?

Because it adds a novel dimension of *personalizing* risk mitigation and control that reflect your individual personality. This new knowledge includes the ability to self-assess one's own most risky online behaviors in a new way. It helps *sensitize* you, and any organization to which you belong, to the likely kinds of third-party cybersecurity hacks and attacks you more easily fall prey to—and to which you must pay particular attention when engaging online.

This knowledge empowers everyone within an organization to self-detect and reflect when they are approaching a risky apex or decision point. Instead of hypervigilance—which as we learned is unsustainable and not always helpful—we can apply *focused awareness*, a condition which *is* sustainable and of real risk-mitigating value. Taking this test helps us detect and avoid situations that are potentially harmful so we worry less about those things that are less likely to be a threat. This brings welcome relief from the constancy of fear that occurs if we believe that all online activity and every act we undertake online is likely to harm or hurt us. The test contours our ability to be empowered against online risks becoming more cyberaware.

The transformative impact of knowledge arising from the test also gives an individual language to compare and share their online behavioral profile with others—family, friends, or colleagues, for instance. As we venture to discuss the *relative risks* of our particular personality and our resulting online behavior, we come to realize that the risks and rewards of being online are variable and uniquely apply to each of us personally. The reduction or elimination of generalized fear and anxiety is a very productive outcome of this approach, enabling a more empowered feeling that contributes, properly, to a now growing sense of online well-being.

While it is clear that no test can entirely eliminate online risk for an individual, it is *entirely predictive* of the kinds of behaviors and attack vectors that are likely to succeed and ensnare you. That is powerful knowledge. And as imperfect as this method is at preventing all harm, isn't it leaps and bounds better than constantly worrying about everything you hear about as a risk online? By enabling online risk assessment in a more self-aware way, you focus on the more relevant threats to you personally and emerge feeling more empowered to be in control.

Worth noting is that this test will **not** detect what someone who has access to your online information might fail to do in securing and protecting access to it. That is simple negligence. And it cannot detect those with criminal intent who are hiding in order to perpetuate fraud or theft—because that is deliberate deviance. This test cannot unmask false intention.

And technology is still imperfect with flaws and failures that can be exploited to hack into systems and steal your information if you have provided it to an organization for any reason. That is never going to change. However, excellent efforts by so many talented cybersecurity professionals are slowly eliminating brute force technology attacks and exploits as the primary source of most cybersecurity breaches today anyway, leaving human hacks as the real threat.

So, this test is aimed at reducing human error—and because we are imperfect—this is the source of more and more of the reported cybersecurity attacks now successfully taking place, and particularly those that involve real economic harm.

Obviously, human-inspired attacks are hard to prevent because they arise from human behavior which is not easily predicted or controlled. Among cybersecurity professionals, it is known these human-factors can never be completely eliminated as a risk. Therefore, any claim by anyone to 100% completely secure systems is impossible to achieve. It is also clear these threats will change and evolve over time, since once we discover one variation and try to eliminate it, creative folks on the other side will come up with a new variant. However, common third-party inspired attacks do fall across a range of established threat vectors today that is useful to understand, each one associated with labels and their own description as follows:

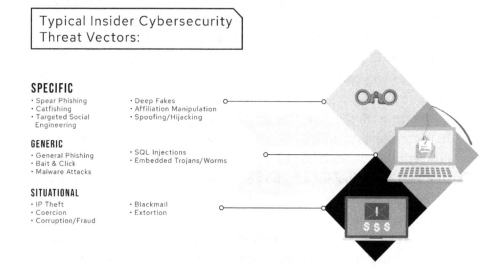

Typical Insider Cybersecurity Threat Vectors:

SPECIFIC
- Spear Phishing
- Catfishing
- Targeted Social Engineering
- Deep Fakes
- Affiliation Manipulation
- Spoofing/Hijacking

GENERIC
- General Phishing
- Bait & Click
- Malware Attacks
- SQL Injections
- Embedded Trojans/Worms

SITUATIONAL
- IP Theft
- Coercion
- Corruption/Fraud
- Blackmail
- Extortion

Most attacks of this sort involve convincing an employee or other insider of an organization, or a family member for that matter, to do something they shouldn't such as providing access to systems through either turning over their credentials, compromising security or password protections, clicking on an attachment that downloads a virus or malware, or being subjected to a deep fake, shaming, or outright extortion for example. In all these instances, *the common weakness that is exploited is human not technical.* You can find lots of additional and up-to-date information on the most current types of online attacks online and from many sources. Of course, just make sure you are getting your information from a reliable source and not being duped by conspiracy theories, false information or being baited by hackers trying to lure you in!

Human factor attacks are often the most damaging kinds of cyber-attacks—because someone always has the "keys to the kingdom" as we say in the tech biz. And if a lock has a key, it can always be opened. If a person can be turned, perhaps even while remaining completely loyal to the organization or with no intent of being exploited, then cyber predators bypass all of the fancy technology protections and often achieve unbridled access to personal information and company secrets. This is what really creates the opportunity for most cybercrimes to occur.

As more organizations recognize this, they learn they cannot continue to rely solely on technology measures to maintain cybersecurity. They then become more interested in this test and other means to help them work with their employees to detect when they are being improperly influenced online. By doing so proactively, they are less likely to trigger a dangerous cybersecurity breach. This is the logical next step in cybersecurity compliance and control even as uncomfortable as this conclusion might be for its human implications. Why?

Because adding a human dimension to compliance and risk management efforts may seem somehow unfair to those being profiled for risk, and this is understandable. But it is not intended to be punitive but constructive and empowering profiling. And any negative feelings cannot stop us from proceeding with this approach either, because not doing something we could do also leaves us feeling uncomfortable, right? We must accept that we are all susceptible to different kinds of risks and online exploitations just because our personalities are all different. The more we know about ourselves, the safer we can make ourselves online.

Further, many of us already take various kinds of other tests to classify us and clarify various things about our aptitudes, skills, and abilities in other areas of our lives. Think about IQ tests, for example. Why not relate it to cybersecurity and our online behaviors?

Ultimately to be more effective, we must stop assuming that profiling without a malicious intent is bad by definition. We must separate inappropriate or misguided profiling—such as racial profiling for example—which we should not do because of its negative societal consequences. It is also inherently unfair and biased. But this test is *not* that kind of profiling.

Instead, it is a helpful tool for both the individual and their organization to deploy so long as it is constructively used to promote safer online practices through awareness and training and not for discriminatory purposes such as hiring and selection. That is because, as you will see for yourself, every single style has value and worth within the organization and is necessary for it to perform properly. Diversity of online style is no different than the many other forms of diversity we promote in organizations that have inherent value. We need to simply accept the risks of everyone's style and improve collective cybersecurity—not for them to leave the organization!

Obviously, I cannot guarantee how people will end up using this test because it is published and available commercially so they can use it however they want to. However, it is my hope that those who take it will enjoy it, learn from it, and benefit from its potential positive impact. But with any new technology, I acknowledge there is always a risk of inappropriate use.

Now that we have discussed the underlying theory of the test itself, let's move on to explore how it can be applied.

By the way, if you are interested in taking the test for yourself please visit **www.cyberconthebook.com** for more information. I am convinced you will be amazed at what you will learn.

CHAPTER THREE:
THE RESULTS

With a new awareness of what your most likely risky behaviors online are, you are empowered to make different choices about how to engage in a rapidly expanding digital world. Instead of blindly falling into whatever the latest trend or online fad is, you can be more reflective about your digital footprint and its value to you (the reward) and compare that with your personal assessment of risk. How might my behavior trigger a bad outcome for me? Based on my profile, am I not detecting an exploit likely intended to take advantage of my personality? This ability makes us feel less afraid, more empowered, and certainly less easily targeted.

While later chapters will explore the organizational implications that arise from the overall findings discovered from the test thus far, at this early stage, let's just focus on something as simple as how you can use it to improve your self-awareness to avoid the most common cybersecurity threats that exist today. To get there, we first need to understand each of the four styles to glean insights on their likely online behaviors.

As with everything else, we know that individuals respond differently to different stimuli and input across varying situations. This means they do not all uniformly behave the same way online either, and so are more or less prone to different kinds of online threats. To understand this better, I mapped the underlying instincts that arise from one's base personality traits in each quadrant to online threats as shown in the illustration below:

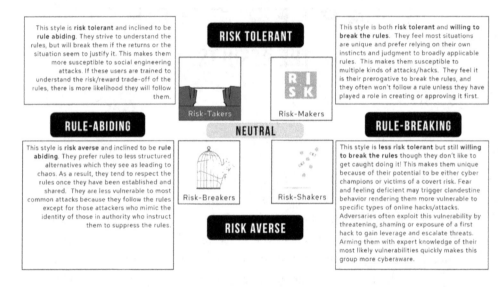

This style is **risk tolerant** and inclined to be **rule abiding**. They strive to understand the rules, but will break them if the returns or the situation seem to justify it. This makes them more susceptible to social engineering attacks. If these users are trained to understand the risk/reward trade-off of the rules, there is more likelihood they will follow them.

RISK TOLERANT

This style is both **risk tolerant** and **willing to break the rules**. They feel most situations are unique and prefer relying on their own instincts and judgment to broadly applicable rules. This makes them susceptible to multiple kinds of attacks/hacks. They feel it is their prerogative to break the rules, and they often won't follow a rule unless they have played a role in creating or approving it first.

RULE-ABIDING

Risk-Takers   Risk-Makers

NEUTRAL

RULE-BREAKING

This style is **risk averse** and inclined to be **rule abiding**. They prefer rules to less structured alternatives which they see as leading to chaos. As a result, they tend to respect the rules once they have been established and shared. They are less vulnerable to most common attacks because they follow the rules except for those attackers who mimic the identity of those in authority who instruct them to suppress the rules.

Risk-Breakers   Risk-Shakers

RISK AVERSE

This style is **less risk tolerant** but still **willing to break the rules** though they don't like to get caught doing it! This makes them unique because of their potential to be either cyber champions or victims of a covert risk. Fear and feeling deficient may trigger clandestine behavior rendering them more vulnerable to specific types of online hacks/attacks. Adversaries often exploit this vulnerability by threatening, shaming or exposure of a first hack to gain leverage and escalate threats. Arming them with expert knowledge of their most likely vulnerabilities quickly makes this group more cyberaware.

The descriptions of these quadrants are pithily summative in nature as any two or three sentence description of someone must be. However, they do attempt to distill the essence of each quadrant as they relate to how cybersecurity threats and innate instincts intersect. And it is the differences among the quadrants that are the most interesting findings from my research.

Today, many organizations either encourage or demand their employees undertake generic cybersecurity risk training. These systems train everyone in the same way to (hopefully) equip them with the same knowledge about cyber threats. The goal is to reduce imminent threats by training employees how to avoid common online risks in the moment. You may even have done some of this training previously at work or in some other context already. There is even some of this available free from various sources such as government or foundations too.

Given all these sources of various best practice "rules" that we should all follow to keep ourselves safe online, and you can likely cite one or more of these rote practices from memory if you have been through any of this type of generic training. But that is exactly the problem—that only indicates simple rote recall. My research proves *it rarely changes your online behavior.*

That is because instincts override training. The likelihood of generic training consistently affecting your online behavior is stunningly low. For a variety of reasons, simply knowing what you *should do* is insufficient to make you *actually do it* although knowing is still better than not. For most of us - except for the risk breakers as described above who really do like to follow the rules once they learn them – just knowing something will not make us do it! But Risk Breakers take pride in this aspect of their underlying personality as it forms a dominant part of their character. For this group of folks, that generic style of rule-based training or awareness is going to work well and is pretty much all that is required. But for the rest of us, not so much.

And because that is also only a percentage of the headcount in any organization—or of the planet's population, for that matter, these methods fail for the 80% or so of people distributed across the other three quadrants. Each style has a varied understanding of the value of risk, reward and rules. They seek different things for different reasons suggesting different techniques are required to actually get them to change their expected behavior. That just makes sense. This can be captured in a chart with simple summary words for each style in terms of what they seek, their preferences, and the methods they use to accomplish personal and work goals as follows:

	SEEKS:	Returns and Rewards
Risk-Takers	PREFERS:	Selective Exceptions
	METHOD:	Contrive

SEEKS:	Innovation and Change
Risk-Makers	PREFERS:	Personal Judgment
METHOD:	Devise

	SEEKS:	Order and Structure
Risk-Breakers	PREFERS:	Compliance with Rules
	METHOD:	Derive

SEEKS:	Sensation and Control
Risk-Shakers	PREFERS:	Autonomy to Choose
METHOD:	Connive

A basic assumption applies across all four quadrants: if our goal is a behavior change either at work or at home, simply telling someone what the best practices are is insufficient incentive and alignment to achieve this change. Perhaps their style sees rules as more akin to guidance or suggestions where they have to contrive or devise new rules to suit their instincts and intentions. Perhaps they feel exceptions to rules can only be derived from the original rule. Or perhaps, they are more conniving, hoping to find a way to break the rules without being detected, making them a covert risk. Maybe they seek change and innovation as stimulation and find following rules boring, or value their own judgement over following a set of standard rules. Among the various styles the test detects, each one seeks different things that excite and motivate, create satisfaction at work and these instincts are absolutely aligned to personality.

Given we now know our individual predilection for risk, reward and rules varies – the conclusion at the very heart of the test itself – means we must rethink much about what we know regarding the human elements of cybersecurity and risk management strategy too. What we thought was working, may not or could be improved. And there are new ways to work that will.

For example, no amount of telling someone who is risk-tolerant that their behavior is putting them at risk is likely to be a sufficient incentive, because of their base personality traits, to have them actually avoiding that risk naturally. A good offline example of that is safe sex practices and how much reinforcement is required before we modify our sexual behaviors. We know these personal choices are accompanied by different levels of risk, yet some people still indulge in risky practices anyway. They both accept higher risk personally as a result and are also more of a risk to others around them in consequence. So why would our online behavior be any different? The mere presence of risk is often insufficient to stop bad behavior.

Similarly, organizations often use a fear-based model outlining all the awful things that could happen if we insist on taking online actions that trigger cybersecurity risks. This overt use of fear to change behavior is a common tactic today and may be summarized best with the phrase we are all just "one click away from cybersecurity disaster," a common meme today.

But this fear-based approach has implications for us both individually and across the whole organization. Not everyone will react the same way to simple possession of knowledge about what kinds of cybersecurity practices can avoid disaster, and the underlying feelings that are provoked by acquiring this information are unpredictable and may have unintended consequences. Therefore, organizations will continue to experience third-party inspired cybersecurity attacks simply because how they are training and educating their workforce is insufficient to entirely avoid risky behaviors. This is because research shows most people are reluctant to believe it will ever happen to them, and so they ignore the training.

For instance, a recent McAfee survey found that *80% of respondents knew* someone who had experienced a cybersecurity attack or hack. Yet, *40% of respondents thought* that the same thing would never happen to them. I wonder in which quadrants some of these folks might find themselves? This finding is also exactly why risk profiling tied to base personality traits is so effective: folks need to understand what is at the root of their unfounded feeling of safety online when they are not, and ensure they accept that being potentially exploited online is a real risk. Instead, people are left to believe, falsely, that it will always happen to someone else, not them.

Further, all training and education suffer from an inherent flaw: humans forget what they have just been taught, often rapidly. The Ebbinghaus Effect, first described in psychological research circa the late 1800s, suggests there is a natural "forgetting curve" that simply makes it impossible to retain everything we learn resulting is as much as 70% of what we learn in a day being forgotten or not actively applied by the next day. So, what defines the 30% we retain and apply? In a context of making cybersecurity training effective, this is an important question.

Research suggests that relevance is an important factor: if we learn something we can immediately apply, we are more likely to retain and use it. There is also the notion that training and development must be a *process,* not an event: we need constant reminders and encouragement to apply what we have learned for it to stick. And finally, repetition. We often need to be told something multiple times before we learn it permanently. Recall how we teach kids to look both ways before they cross the street to understand this particular point. So one-time training is an insufficient strategy for the average human of any age to acquire, retain, and apply new knowledge.

The dirty secret of the industry is that Big Tech knows this too. They know full well cybersecurity is a human problem. But they just keep on selling us more technology anyway, knowing their promises of it being "secure" and "safe" hinge on an unreliable assumption of human compliance with instructions that is patently false. Users do *not* always follow the rules even if they have been taught them, and even if they fear negative consequences. Why is this?

Let's consider an offline analogy to explore this point. You buy something that requires assembly, and it comes with instructions. For the purposes of this example to follow, I am equating assembly instructions to company "rules," "policies," or "procedures" for the purposes. Intuitively, this example clearly demonstrates how people approach this situation differently. In my consulting practice and speeches, I often refer to this explanation as the Ikea Effect! So, you are opening the recently arrived box of new furniture before assembling it…

Do you read the manual thoroughly from beginning to end before starting assembly? Maybe you are afraid that if you don't get it right from the beginning, a furniture assembly disaster looms? If so, the test will likely identify you as a Risk-Breaker located in the lower-left quadrant. Or maybe you are an instruction skimmer who seeks sufficient superficial understanding in your view to mitigate the risk of bad assembly. But your desire to get the job done and the furniture assembled (a tactic that delivers the reward of the new furniture faster in your mind) makes you more likely a Risk-Taker located in the upper left quadrant.

While both of these styles have a variance in terms of risk tolerance, they are similar in terms of a willingness to follow the rules to some extent, both falling on the left side of the horizontal axis in my model. Each considered the instructions to some degree, just in different levels of detail and speed in application and consistency, accepting the risks of that decision.

If you just open the box and start assembling whatever it is, while the instructions remain unread, the test indicates you as a Risk-Maker located in the upper right quadrant. You inherently believe your past experience, regardless of the degree to which it applies, equips you to assemble this piece of furniture. You do not need written instructions provided by someone else to help, trusting your own judgment and instincts instead. We all know someone like this!

Finally, if you are a Risk-Shaker, you always want to *project* confidence that you understand the task at hand, even if you feel a bit daunted by the undertaking. So the fear of looking foolish either forces you to read the manual thoroughly to become a true expert, bestowing upon you "mover and shaker status – pun intended – or you take shortcuts to glean just enough information to present self-confidence while actually remaining quite shaky about just what to do.

Of course the end product furniture will turn out vastly different depending on your choice: either a perfectly assembled, model piece of furniture that is an outstanding example of clever proficiency and skill or a lop-sided contraption that is hardly recognizable as a piece of furniture and ultimately quite useless. Regardless, Risk-Shakers will defend to the death that the real cause of the disaster was the *manufacturer,* not their own shakiness of course! That is because they don't like to be detected and prefer their failures to remain covert.

To be fair to all the quadrants, this analogy is of practical importance to establishing that our online behavior, risky or not, is actually a reflection of our underlying base personality traits and is not random. And it is a bit more nature than it is nurture when interpreted from this perspective. Further, we all probably have a little bit of some of the traits of each quadrants in us at various times and in various ways for the science of personality is far from completely reliable. So again, none of the four approaches is "better" than any other, and each ends in the furniture being assembled somehow, someway.

Of course, over time as experience intrudes and shapes our worldview, that affects our personality and conduct within that world. We learn over time to mitigate bad consequences for ourselves from behavior that, while it was innate, did not serve us well. So, we strive to be in control of that behavior through the benefit of experience. That is not the same as being afraid.

In the case of the assembly of the purchase in question, IF we have done this before and found that it was less than successful—perhaps we gave up in frustration, something had to be undone and re-done the right way, or perhaps we irretrievably broke the purchase beyond repair—that experience helps shape our future behavior in future situations to some extent. This awareness helps us suppress our natural instincts in favor of behavior that will benefit us more.

In theory, but not in practice, the same thing should apply to our online behavior. We should become more experienced and better versed in the online tradeoffs between the risks and rewards of our underlying instincts borne of our innate personality style. It should cause us to examine our actual online behavior. However, that assumes that the threat vectors and technology realms in which we function also remain relatively stable such that we can apply that experience forward from one situation to the next. Unfortunately, technology changes so quickly that the half-life of our technology grows shorter each day as new apps, new features, and entirely new platforms become available and are deployed. This makes our online world one of the few in which our nature is far more likely to prevail on first instinct than our experience.

This makes the finding of the test that much more important as a fundamental tool to self-equip us with knowledge that can make us more risk-aware, but without inducing an overwhelming level of fear for that is unproductive. Fear actually prevents the joy that would otherwise happen if we accept the risks of participation, a recurring theme in my research.

I am not personally inclined to believe risk is best minimized through non-participation, in technology or anything else. Regardless, this is often not possible (i.e., you must be online to do your job, or you choose to be online because it offers you some advantage that you prefer to enjoy), or more likely, can attract another consequence of potential social isolation. Let's face it: in today's interconnected world, technology is both a great enabler and a great disabler.

To leave yourself out in response to fear will deprive you of any or all benefit that technology might offer. On the other hand, having a cybersecurity profile that suggests indiscriminately diving into every new online platform, device, or app is also not a good trait either. As with many things in life, we use our self-awareness, our savvy, and some degree of self-control to reflect on our choices before acting on any of them to ensure an optimal balance of risk and reward appropriate to each of us.

To help achieve this mission, CyberconIQ has developed specific approaches to training that are aligned with these inherent cybersecurity personalities. We simply refer to this as "style-aligned training", and it works. In detecting your likely online behavior from the test, we can then align training messages and methods to better accomplish the objective of the training which is designed to affect actual online and on-the-job behavior. While an important achievement, it flows naturally from the obvious assumption that because we are all different, demonstrating different personalities, we will all respond differently to varying types of training about the various kinds of cybersecurity risks that exist and which may be leveled at us when we are participating online. That is one point of differentiation.

Each of the four quadrants will also experience a different success rate from different types of third-party inspired attacks, and they will prevail or not based on the ability of the individual to either predict or detect that they are being targeted and then interdicting their own behavior to avert the risk. There is absolutely no technology that can prevent this type of attack all of the time, although filtering systems do help and are absolutely necessary. These tools are only able able to prevent *known* malicious messages from reaching into the network perhaps or alerting users with warning messages and the like in the hopes that higher user awareness will result in an unsuccessful attack. But at the end of the day, we are absolutely relying on a single individual, with an inherently unique style, to hopefully behave in such a way as to avoid doing something which benefits the bad guys instead of us. In other words, often we are just one click away from disaster, a fact that drives fear. So we need to resolve this dread somehow.

For those working in cybersecurity professionally, wouldn't it be nice to be able to profile individuals on some legal kind of basis that *may indicate* a greater likelihood of risk for the most common threat vectors used to attack us? Wouldn't that help prevent attacks? And empower others to thwart attacks? For instance, we observe that men are more prone to be risk-takers than women generally, for all kinds of intriguing reasons. There is no point in debating the validity of this conclusion because it is a biological fact and I do not make this statement for any sexist purpose or to be socially provocative at all. If we were honest with ourselves, gender would be a factor in assessing one's risk of a cybersecurity attack, of course.

In some instances, there may be other predictable factors such as age, loosely translating to experience, that may also have a statistical correlation indicating younger and less experienced people may be more at risk of online exploitation than those who are older and have more experience. That might seem to make sense and be a valid assumption. Or maybe it's the other way, and younger, more technologically savvy employees are less vulnerable than older employees who are not part of the internet-native generations?

Perhaps religion, country of origin, race, or some other demographic factor might also demonstrate correlation to one being more of a cybersecurity risk. Or, perhaps, the education, perspective, or cultural attributes you possess offers some insight into potential ways a person could be exploited more easily online. For instance, maybe you believe in helping others because of a deeply held religious belief arising from biblical references to Jesus' humility. While this may be a good instinct, it is easily detected online in many instances and may be an easily exploitable weakness as far as the cybercriminals who will use it against you are concerned.

BUT STOP. If you do not already feel squeamish, you should carefully consider what you just read more carefully. While those examples are clear and you may wish to consider them personally for any awareness of cybersecurity risk they may offer, can you imagine any workplace profiling employees on any of those factors? Obviously, both the law (for instance, various equal opportunity and anti-discrimination acts in the United States and other jurisdictions such as the EEOC) and ethics likely completely prevent this as an approach to mitigating risks of a cybersecurity attack even were it to work. Flat out, this is just not a solid approach to risk mitigation and management, unless you are perhaps working in an intelligence agency with discretion to use these kinds of criteria to detect domestic terrorists, as we will explore later in this book. But organizationally, it would never be appropriate to profile on any of these factors.

That is why my test is so different: it does **not** rely on any demographic factor that is prohibited by law or by ethical practice. It is psychologically non-invasive, and respondents actually report the test as being easy to do, fun to complete, and not disturbing in any respect. While personal in nature, it detects *job-relevant* approaches to risk, reward, and rules. This makes it perfectly legal to expect employees to undertake this test for that valid purpose. Now, some companies will still resist this simply because of it being a test—but how about the much bigger fear of cyber breach? That is a very real threat and imposes massive consequences on any company and its customers, something to truly fear!

And the costs of cybersecurity compliance are growing daily as the range of human-factor threats and attacks increase exponentially. These are not as easily identified and eliminated, making compliance with consumer expectations of privacy and security even harder to achieve in practice. When every member of the team, no matter how well-intentioned, loyal, or capable can be targeted and potentially exploited, what are we to do? Should we simply go offline? I somehow doubt that; so instead, we need to find as sophisticated a way to defend ourselves in practice and as quickly as the predators exhibit new ways to exploit us as prey.

How can we best accomplish that? Self-awareness that leads to a positive feeling can empower us to detect and prevent ourselves from becoming the weak link in the chain. That way, we overcome a fear-based view of cybersecurity and replace it with a sense of becoming a tribe of cyber warriors, ready to defend ourselves when attacked by ensuring that we have the right knowledge ahead of time. This means understanding what kinds of attacks the enemy is likely to deploy, how we intend to defend ourselves and ensuring the highest possible degree of compliance with tactics that avoid a successful attack on our organization. Personal knowledge as offense is our best organizational defense, suggesting a discriminated basis for training, development, and selective systems controls focused on the highest risks is the best approach.

Showing up in a quadrant that demonstrates a more likely statistical risk for a successful cybersecurity attack of a specific type is *not* bad in and of itself. That is because, as I stated before, the corollary to that is the necessity for all styles across all four quadrants for the DNA of the organization to remain intact and functioning at peak performance, and someone in any quadrant can be hacked. But we still need everyone on-board! Being resistant to understanding how our personal behavior and online inclinations may be contributing to a tendency of being exploited by others for illicit gain is bad—it's denial actually—and can lead to disastrous outcomes. That's where I really think the self-awareness arising from taking the test and completing style-aligned training, in addition, becomes a corporate program with the practical ability to radically reduce human-factor-related cybersecurity risks.

Consider the example of a stock, commodity, or currency trader at a bank. Again, by obvious definition, these folks must be risk-tolerant and able to make instantaneous risk/reward tradeoff decisions on their clients' behalf. Of course, we would not want these folks to entirely be devoted to a rule-based view of the world because of the nonlinear markets in which they operate: they must be able to use their instincts and skills to react to the market, not try and impute a rule to follow that will always apply and make them successful. Practically speaking, we could not operate a bank successfully without some risk seekers in our midst.

However, those same folks would perhaps not be terrific at audit, compliance, or risk management functions because of the necessity to strictly interpret and follow rules consistently which is not an inherent strength of this style. By nature, employees attracted to these functions likely exhibit a different orientation toward rules and to demonstrate more compliance and due process tendencies rather than assuming the prerogative of their own individual creativity or judgment instead. They like rules. Of course, as I developed the test, I became deeply aware of these distinctions because, in larger pilots, one could immediately detect similarities in the quadrants that, generally speaking, certain types of job categories reflected.

While the pattern is not always absolute and exceptions always exist, it was apparent often enough to be statistically valid, confirming that all organizations benefit from the contributions of all quadrants and that no one style is superior to another. Therefore, the emphasis should not be on eliminating any style simply for the sake of reducing risk without knowing it will also reduce rewards. Just like in real life—it takes all types to make the world go 'round, and so it is across these four styles in organizations.

That said, if an organization knew for a fact that some groups were more at risk than others for certain types of cyberattacks, might it intervene in those instances differently? Might it train those employees differently, or subject them to different controls that might inhibit such an attack from being successful? All done with a lens of reducing total organizational risk and not targeting individuals, of course. And would such a differentiated response that might seem unfair if it was not universal, suddenly seem quite fair and reasonable if the employees concerned knew their individual and collective cybersecurity profiles and the aggregate risk that this represented for the company if it did not act accordingly?

Better still, could we engage employees in discussions among themselves about their individual profiles and inherent approach to risk, reward, and rules and then ask them to self-develop strategies to mitigate this risk that they may be more willing to follow for instance? This now makes collective cybersecurity the mission of the entire organization, the holy grail of cybersecurity professionals everywhere.

On that same topic, in developing and testing our style-compliant training, we discovered something interesting. As we obviously needed to modify the themes and approach to training for each quadrant if we expected on-the-job behavior to change, we determined that at its core there was a **single dominant set of behaviors** that worked best to defeat third-party inspired cyberattacks. A core methodology involving getting people to stop and think basically.

To encapsulate that easily for learners, we developed a memorable tagline for our company—"Save yourself from yourself". That is derived from core behaviors we identified everyone needs to demonstrate all the time, both at work and at home, as follows:

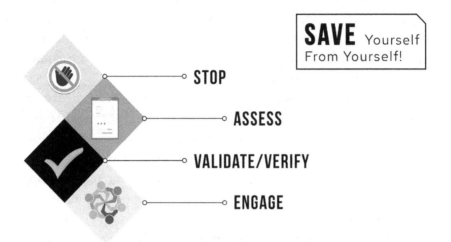

These steps operate exactly as you would expect: first-off, STOP and do not let a false sense of urgency or trickery force you into doing something you should not. Pause long enough to apply all steps. Then ASSESS what you are being asked, prompted or instructed to do: is this a normal, recurring task you are familiar with or something new and unexpected. How likely is this to be real you must ask yourself?

The two next steps are intertwined and are more situationally-adjusted to what you are facing. However, they basically involve reassuring yourself that you have *independently* VALIDATED and VERIFIED what you are doing and why, including doubling back and certifying every instruction and actor to ensure it is legit and true. Finally, before executing any step to its final conclusion, have you ENGAGED sufficiently in exploring your own instincts and vulnerabilities – and if not who else might you ask for help – and invoked all necessary steps to the best of your ability to ENSURE you are not being hacked?

These five simple steps, if consistently applied, virtually eliminate 100% of likely exploits used in the most common types of third-party inspired cybersecurity attacks. This approach can keep us all safer! But getting everyone to apply these consistently in every situation is challenging because of these inherent personality differences. That is because so many of these external attackers rely on exploiting an intention to create a false sense of urgency, making unrealistic promises about returns or rewards, or exploiting our differing human natures to perpetuate these fraudulent attacks in the first place, often by gaining false trust or using empty threats.

You can now easily surmise how the different styles across the four quadrants might respond if we simply tell them this is what they should do. Do you think they will do it? We know they won't. Instead, we need to personalize this message in unique ways that inspire people to connect their personal traits to the ways they get targeted and bring awareness to the rules and how they particularly need to implement them for themselves.

And it works. The rates at which people comply using style-aligned training dramatically increases compliance, just exactly what this book contemplates as a solution to the ever-present challenge of a human-inspired cybersecurity breach that happens outside the direct control of technology professionals. The tool and training actually elevate the internal discussions in companies from being fear-based to hopeful and empowering. As a result of acquiring new knowledge about themselves, employees act and behave differently and start to appreciate the *need* to behave differently online in order to keep the organization safe. By shifting the conversation internally, we advance the cybersecurity culture throughout the organization and gain collective insight and cooperation toward more inspired compliance. Cybersecurity becomes a "team sport" when everyone aspires to play together more effectively.

Restoring Hope: Cybersecurity as a Team Sport

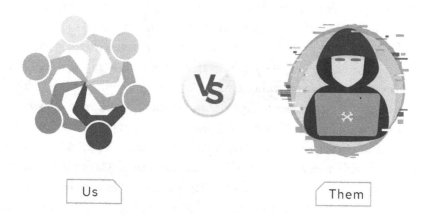

Us

Them

Since the tool permits anyone to reliably self-assess their level of cybersecurity risk, they gain sensitivity to the importance of their own responsibility for cybersecurity in a profoundly personal way—*they get it*. How do we know? Post-test surveys confirm improved awareness and willingness to comply with new behaviors at a much higher rate than before taking the test, and at a rate superior to generic training. There was also higher recall of lessons learned and higher awareness of how to consistently apply them in the workplace.

More important, within days of completing the test and training, further proof emerged, including lower rates of incidents of compromise or concern (IOCs) and reduced failure rates on individual follow-up social penetration testing and retesting. These assessments capture direct impact on company-wide risk levels indicating a higher ROI for these methods compared to traditional, generic approaches to cybersecurity training. I surmise much of this has to do with increased cyberawareness and to feeling more empowered to avoid personal online risks.

These results also have much to do with instilling a collective culture inside the organization, making it okay to be vulnerable, but *not* okay to ignore the collective impact of that personal realization on others. This sensitization effect has long been understood to arise when we learn something new. As we acquire knowledge and an accompanying language to describe complex psychological phenomena in new ways, it sparks comparative dialogue among us.

An offline example can help: have you ever been sitting innocently with a partner or friend—maybe watching TV or hanging out? As is so often the case, a smartphone or tablet is not far out of reach, maybe even being used together to surf the web, lurk on social media, listen to music, or watch videos. Eventually, your companion is attracted to some new online survey, questionnaire, app, or some such. And BAM: you are ensnared with a request to also do the same thing. Maybe it claims to answer questions such as: "are we truly a compatible couple?", "are we meant to be best friends forever?", or "what will you be like or look like as you age?". Whatever the meme meant to be explored, in completing this experience together in real-time, we are almost forced to share the results. We become aware of things about ourselves, perhaps funny and true or not, that nonetheless spark a dialogue on a topic that was not chosen so much as imposed on each participant as a result of having been exposed to the test. And you are both instantly more sensitive and sensitized to the topic and its impact on your perceptions.

So, it is with the impact of the human elements of cybersecurity when explored in this new way. The internal dialogue among colleagues is permanently changed after taking this test and the organization as a whole experiences a *positive sensitization effect* about how individual behavior can lead to improved collective cybersecurity outcomes.

This is a powerful soft outcome that cannot be underestimated for its immediate impact on advancing the cybersecurity culture. It works in any context – family or workplace –because taking the test together generates new awareness simply by introducing new language into group conversations about cybersecurity. That has beneficial effects on reducing fear, increasing empowerment, and reducing risky outcomes that matter to everyone individually, within families, as an organization or around the world even. And that is my personal mission.

C H A P T E R   F O U R :
TONE FROM THE TOP

While much of this book applies both personally and professionally, the larger-impact events in cybersecurity mostly happen in larger organizations because the scale and nature of potential damage is just simply that much higher. This implies a necessary focus in any organization on proactively managing cybersecurity risk, a mounting worry and growing cost for business executives and owners that is unsustainable. I worry that if we can't get wrest control of this situation shortly, the looming economic harm of cybersecurity threats will eventually overwhelm the positive human, social and business impacts of the internet for us all.

So cybersecurity remains incredibly important for organizations—from the small one-person doctor's office that contains vitally sensitive and personal health information to the world's largest global bank. This means every CEO, owner, or even elected leader of any organization of any type must be completely cyberaware today, ready to lead his or her organization in learning how to collectively keep the organization safer online. We must transform cybersecurity into a "team sport" by which I mean a collective concern for every member of any organization, stimulated and supported as a common goal by leadership.

In our consulting practice, we refer to this as "tone from the top." And it equally applies to Big Tech itself where, as consumers with more collective clout than we actually imagine we have, we can demand that the CEOs of these social media behemoths start to walk the talk instead of just talk the talk when it comes to the risks we have explored in this book.

Will the tone from the top across Big Tech shift to take responsibility for the negative consequences their platforms impose on the safety and security of us all? And will Congress—and political leadership at the top of nations around the world—finally get it and start to impose regulatory action and other appropriate steps to hold Big Tech accountable for paying its fair share of taxes and behaving more justly for the greater good, for instance? That would be a significant and positive change in the current anti-tech climate where the chorus of frustrated voices of consumers is growing daily. Society is concerned, and rightly so.

But as we have learned thus far, this is *not* uniquely a technology issue either. Therefore, we must accept some co-responsibility for where we are. And that means the problem cannot simply be deferred to those in the organization responsible for technology and information security. That's just too simple. Although that might help reduce fear and, especially if you are at the top of your organization, may make you feel like you put an expert in charge of something that scares you, this alone will not protect you. It is a false sense of security that is actually contributing to the misappropriation of this problem as being technology-based instead of being properly seen as a strategic human capital and leadership issue.

The responsibility for keeping organizations safe and out of harm's way—online or offline—is the responsibility of *all leaders across an organization* under the guidance of someone at the top. My research has discovered that tone from the top is ultimately one of *the most important factors* that determines how successfully an organization can collectively predict and interdict risky human behavior, both individually and collectively. This is a vital finding.

The courageous act by leadership of changing the conversation about cybersecurity inside their organization to make it both more real, but also less frightening, is measurably shown to improve cyber-security outcomes through positive changes in on-the-job compliance behavior.

So how does a leader make this happen? It begins with assessment and acceptance of the innate characteristics of the employees you lead, either within your direct sphere of influence or across the whole organization. People are different, and they exhibit different traits and tendencies. This makes managing the human elements of cybersecurity complex because each of us exhibit different instincts when we are online making us more or less prone to being exploited in different ways by third-party inspired cyberattacks and hacks.

What changes with this new knowledge—and particularly when we ask all employees to take this test to self-determine their cybersecurity risk profile—*is that we reduce fear and replace it with hope*. Finally, we have an opportunity to secure a way of understanding ourselves and how we can *personally contribute every day* to keeping ourselves and our organization safer.

In addition, the organization acquires new language to talk about how we interact with the forces online and offline that want to harm us by inducing us to behave in ways that compromise security and safety. Most organizations' approach to cybersecurity—and enterprise risk management generally—is fear-based: we spell out the consequences of a successful cybersecurity attack, define guidelines and results that we expect everyone one of our employees to follow, secure our digital borders from intruders as best we can, and then hope and pray this all works to keep us safe and off the front pages of the newspaper! Remember Equifax anyone?

So that won't work. Our current approach is nearing the limits of its ROI already, and the sheer and growing number of breaches and the growing costs of compliance are not yielding the results organizations need to make customers and clients feel safe. And they are losing trust.

One must recognize that a fear-based approach leads employees to an unwanted state of hypervigilance and/or hyperarousal that is not sustainable, and ultimately unproductive. In fact, the constant hyping of fear of the consequences of an attack can paralyze an organization and render it into a state of complacency rather than compliance—a worse state of affairs exposing your organization to undetected levels of human risk that no technology solution can prevent.

One just needs to look at the rapidly rising incidence rates of cybersecurity breaches to be assured that even as cybersecurity spending increases globally, successful attacks are more frequent. My hypothesis to explain this is fatigue-induced complacency.

So, instead of giving in to instinctual or institutionalized fear, I recommend leaders change the tone of their organization's internal conversation. Transform it from fear to hope by empowering the organization to take its cybersecurity destiny into its own hands. As a leader, you need to demonstrate the courage to take this conversation in a new direction, away from fear alone, and instill hope that by collaborating and by being both aware of and respectful of each other's unique online styles, we can all help each other improve collective cybersecurity. To do so involves technology, process and people all working productively together:

Most organizations focus on technology and risk-controlled process designs as their primary risk mitigation tools. Yet, their higher risk is people-based and less predictable. A cyber-based view of the firm tackles total cybersecurity risk from an integrated perspective targeting management attention on the people elements first!

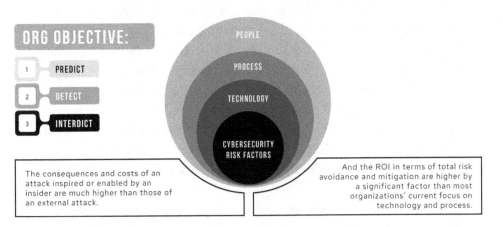

ORG OBJECTIVE:

1 PREDICT

2 DETECT

3 INTERDICT

PEOPLE

PROCESS

TECHNOLOGY

CYBERSECURITY RISK FACTORS

The consequences and costs of an attack inspired or enabled by an insider are much higher than those of an external attack.

And the ROI in terms of total risk avoidance and mitigation are higher by a significant factor than most organizations' current focus on technology and process.

Having piloted this instrument in multiple different organizations and contexts, I have learned that the mere introduction of the test itself into an organization alters the tack and tone of these internal conversations, and starts to positively influence the internal risk culture.

To see how that works in practice, let's step outside of the online world for a second and return to the offline world and its more normal state of social interaction among people. If you are married or dating, have you ever done one of those fun personality or couples-matching tests that suggest they can determine your degree of compatibility with your spouse or partner? Maybe you were sitting on the couch, watching TV or a movie, and it is innocently suggested you should take this test to see what it says. So, you do. And the test is revealing, if not reliable and as you both digest what it says, you begin to converse.

Without the triggering event of the test delivering a result, and the accompanying language it provides for you to both understand and talk about your life as a couple, it seems unlikely the topic would have come up in that moment and in that way. Psychologically, this act of taking the test sensitizes you to phenomena you were perhaps either unaware of, or even in denial about. Important to note, not all of these have to be bad things you discover just because they lurk under the surface. Good discoveries about one's self are also made in these same moments, and a balanced interpretation is essential. That is also one of the reasons I worked so hard in extracting the findings from the test into *positive and validating* profiles so that everyone detects positive value in their own style and its place in the organization.

So, this same impact is created when an organization adopts my cybersecurity testing and profiling system. It provides access to standardized language that helps define complicated trait-based risk concepts for your employees, while also giving them permission to talk amongst themselves about collective cybersecurity across the organization in a new way.

In our team's consulting work, we found value in simply having people share their indicated profile type and to seek out others in the organization who are both the same and different to explore how these differing styles coalesce organization-wide. Dialogue across organizational functions also improves collective ownership of new initiatives, reducing overall cybersecurity risk for the firm. This is an important breakthrough not possible unless you have a positive cybersecurity-related event that provokes accompanying new conversations to occur.

Without disclosing this ambition specifically, good leaders will embrace what has just been described as a subtle form of subtle change management. As these new cybersecurity conversations seep into the organization, an important culture shift occurs that is beneficial to overall cyberawareness. And sensitization across the organization drives higher compliance.

Furthermore, as the internal state of hyperarousal/hypervigilance is reduced, people see a new path forward that enables them to feel more in control of their own behavior. This reduces fatigue-based complacency by empowering them to feel like they can actively contribute to keeping the organization secure online even while positively reducing their own stress. This is a dual win: individual employee stress is lowered while organizational harm is measurably reduced by mitigating the likelihood of a successful cybersecurity attack occurring.

This virtuous cycle is highly valuable to your current cybersecurity efforts. And it all starts with the correct tone from the top that drives a detectable shift in the conversation to gently shape the culture toward voluntary compliance through more enthusiasm and team attention to action. Instead of being fear-driven, you spark a more sustainable change in behavior and create a sense of collective destiny that "the bad guys are just <u>not</u> gonna win around here!" Again, cybersecurity becomes a team sport, with hope and enthusiasm that we can all win at this.

Contrast that with how organizations approach cybersecurity today. Maybe you have already invested in generic individual cybersecurity training, for example. It tests your employees for their knowledge of dangerous practices and trains them how to behave differently, maybe followed up by fake attacks to check for compliance, right? Are you surprised by how many individuals still fall prey to, for instance, a fake phishing e-mail scheme after all that? Or those who still click on unknown attachments even after being trained not to? Why so?

Ultimately, generic training does not acknowledge what we can now recognize as the most important aspect of any cybersecurity intervention: it is not personalized sufficiently to actually drive a deep change in personal behavior because, in the heat of the moment with the state of heightened fear that is present, any human's base instincts will prevail. And generic training alone doesn't make it okay to seek help from others when individuals come to critical decision points, because that is a cultural shift in tone from the top.

Quite simply, some of your employees are more instinctively prone to taking risks and breaking rules and no amount of repetitive generic training will change that. Yet, we cannot eliminate them from the organization either because we would then also eliminate their contributions and value to organizational performance. Instead, we must develop self-awareness that guides them to self-train about what changes in behavior *they agree make sense for them,* and that will actually help them contribute to keeping the organization safer. We must appeal to their base instincts.

This works in practice because employees actually do want to help and contribute to organizational success. They care and want to be recognized for doing the right things. But there is also this question of instinct and style embedded in our personalities which makes any organization so challenging for leaders to manage: because people are all different. And they respond differently. So how we approach questions of cybersecurity must also be different.

In making this observation, which I know from experience works, I am not dismissing that there is a large body of accumulated knowledge about what kinds of attacks (threat vectors) and what kinds of defenses we need in place (mitigation) among employees that can stop most third-party inspired attacks from becoming successful. Nor do I reject technology tools that look for signatures and patterns that can prevent large numbers of fake e-mails from reaching your employees in the first place. These are all solid and fundamentally correct steps to put in place that contribute to organizational cybersecurity levels. But these efforts all initially relate to knowledge acquisition rather than to unique personality instincts, which must be addressed first before knowledge can be successfully and consistently applied.

We know there are always going to be new forms of attack, from new sources that involve new ways of compromising us. We cannot always anticipate those and avoid them all. This means no technology can prevent all attacks at the system level. That is a fool's errand.

Rather, we should try and stop them by focusing organizational resources on the other 80% of the equation by adding as much emphasis on the human side of our organization whenever we make investments in cybersecurity prevention. What are we doing to facilitate how employees *feel* about always being afraid? What can we do about that? Can we help them channel this anxiety into *hope* that the organizations' efforts really can prevail and will keep it safe? How do we delve into much of what we have discovered in this book and turn it into style-aligned training and support that speaks directly not just to the safe online practices—the point of cybersecurity training—but also to ways that this training can be turned into coaching and adoption that increases the likelihood that their on-the-job behavior at that moment when we most need it to be different will, in fact, be different? That cybersecurity conundrum is real.

And what makes the approach framed in this book fundamentally different from what organizations are already doing? It starts with acknowledging personal instincts first before trying to force feed necessary knowledge into someone. Need I remind any reader of the Equifax attack – once again – to understand just how randomly a cybersecurity breach can ruin an entire company's brand and reputation in an instant? *These kinds of attacks are successful because of a single click by a single employee in a single moment in time.* That attack went undetected for five and a half months and involved the compromising of more than 170 million Americans' critical information including financial and personal data completely useful to criminals that want to steal your identity.

So the focus of this book is how, in that moment, we can all prevent that single click and ensure reliance on the team to share the opportunity to check in with each other—a gut check validation if you will—that is the most vital, frontline defense we have. As you saw previously in chapter three, we use our SAVE acronym in all our training as a reminder to constantly protect ourselves from our own bad online habits and instincts.

When employees support each other—directly and without judgment—because that is "the way things are around here"—a leader has engaged the human side of cybersecurity to make the mission of keeping the organization safer one everyone does together. Meaningful progress.

The playful banter, teasing and true appreciation for each style that my consulting team and I witness every time we apply this test and undertake training and coaching sessions with employees helps prove why this approach is both so different and gratifying to share. Employees report, for likely the first time ever, feeling like a tribe of cyberwarriors—in a good and empowering way—able to defend themselves and their organization from cyberattacks and the harm and havoc they inflict. They willingly do so now, no longer out of fear or duty, but out of optimism and hope that their efforts really do matter and will be successful. It becomes about true progress, achieved just one click at a time, that make us all feel safer online.

Of course, to get there, first we have to overcome a couple of natural reactions: the first is test anxiety. Many folks are prone to this and feel as if they will somehow not perform up-to-par or that they have to give the test the "right answers" that management must be looking for. To correct this in practice, we have often suggested that the senior leadership team pilot the test among themselves first, understand it from the inside out, and then fully disclose their own styles and what they have personally learned from taking the test and the training.

In turn, this builds confidence that the test is *not* seeking the right answers **from you,** but rather the right answers **for you.** Properly taken, the test gives you a *personal* result and summarizes information that everyone should want to know about themselves. No style is a bad style, and all styles are valuable and required for the organization to function. We need risk-takers in some areas as much as we need rule followers and there is no balance that is "right" for the organization. In fact, the dispersion across the styles truly does vary collectively and is not statistically predictable. That suggests that different organizations will have different combinations of people on their teams which have likely evolved over time to match the mission of the organization, the hiring skills and tendencies of leaders, and the culture in terms of fit between employees and company.

The other issue that testing invokes is often raised by HR: isn't the test going to invade employees' privacy and feel intrusive? The answer is no. For the most part, anyone taking the test—which now as a reader of this book includes you—will see that it is benign, non-invasive, and does not actually even seem difficult for most people to take. It's forty simple questions and all in simple language that is easy to interpret for most folk. Of course, the scoring mechanisms are complex, and the method used to get from answers to these simple questions generating a profile is the patented secret of the test. And test-takers mostly report that the test is not psychologically invasive and is very easy to take.

It is also completely legal for employers to use because, as indicated in earlier chapters, it does not depend on any demographic or personal information to be valid. Full disclosure: this also renders the test more relevant to predicting and detecting on-the-job behaviors more so than one's personal, at-home risk/rule behaviors. We all know someone who seems to demonstrate a certain kind of demeanor and personality at work and who is completely different at home. For others, the two places offer a fairly consistent expression of personality. This is actually unimportant to the conclusion of the test, particularly as leaders in the organization. All we want the test to do is provoke the conversation change—from fear to hope-based—that then leads to a reduction in harm to our employees by helping negate the constant sense of hypervigilance and fear, and which measurably improves both changes in on-the-job behavior that matter to our cybersecurity results, and which bring us one click closer to safety rather than compromise.

As leaders representing an employer, we do not particularly care about the risk/reward/rule trade-offs our employees make at home, on vacation, or with friends and family. Of course, for many, the information they gain from the test will also positively impact their cybersecurity at home as well, and they may even be inclined to share this tool with family members to seek the same positive impact they have experienced in their workplace. That is how powerfully positive gaining this knowledge is for most employees—they feel good about it.

I urge CEOs I work with to ensure a tone from the top that enshrines the principle that *all styles* are valuable and important and *all employees regardless of style* are responsible for improving our team's cybersecurity and compliance results. We do not use the test to "blame" any particular style. We embrace all styles and understand that it is diversity on the team that makes us strong, high-performing, and ready to take on this challenge. Emphasize that every single member of the team is important and necessary for the effort to succeed.

Employees are often comforted when this is reinforced. They become less resistant to the idea of taking the test and embrace the risk profile it produces as a valuable personal tool. Sometimes our clients will offer employees the chance to take the test anonymously or to not have the results shared with their employer, an option we offer. While this may seem an intriguing option—and our test management system offers it to our clients—we try and convince employers to take the calculated risk of making this a mandatory part of being on the team but using completely reassuring language about that intent. And it can work.

We want to achieve what we call *collaborative cybersecurity awareness* and to take this challenge on as a team, leaders included. We all need new knowledge and approaches. By taking the test and training, sharing the results, and changing the dialogue within your team or across the company, you ultimately get a more highly aware and engaged workforce all ready, willing, and able to do whatever it takes to keep us all safe online. This outcome cannot be accomplished if we are afraid of the information we might learn. So we must repurpose this anxiety and embrace the test as a way of gaining cybersecurity advantage over those who want to harm us.

While this chapter is geared more toward leaders in an organization, it should also bring comfort to any employee, anywhere in the organization, and even personally. Improved knowledge about our inherent human tendencies and traits, and how those fit into the workplace behavior both positively and negatively, should be something we all seek to understand. This tool—a breakthrough on the human factors side of cybersecurity and compliance—should not be feared. It is only intended to be informative and constructive.

When used by skilled leaders, it can change the conversation and culture around compliance and truly transform your organization's risk profile by making cybersecurity everybody's business, every day and in completely new and effective ways. It can make cybersecurity a team sport that we all play and win together to help keep us all safer online.

CHAPTER FIVE:
WHY CAN'T I JUST BUY CYBERINSURANCE?

Because that won't keep you entirely safe online either! Cybersecurity insurance is certainly available and is a booming business. And there are lots of other online products and services designed to help you monitor for identity theft, prevent unauthorized personal credit, lockdown your home title, or hunt for leaked personal information for sale on the dark web. None of these products is good or bad in and of themselves. But they are only tools to mitigate expanding cybersecurity threats, not to eliminate them entirely. So, is this just more false hope?

Before addressing the complicated question of insuring against cyber risks, let's explore the simpler question of the real value offered to consumers by various services designed to help increase your personal online security. When one is afraid—even subconsciously—and in a heightened state of awareness about pending risks, one of the things that tempts us into feeling better is to transfer or share that risk somehow. It comforts us. This was the essence of our early tribal nature as humans: by not going it alone and instead joining together in collectives that helped each other, ease of life and survival rates increased and our anxiety about living in a dangerous world decreased. This is the whole point of insurance—risk transfer.

As someone who has studied both online behaviors and also the various kinds of tools and services being used to manage cybersecurity risk, I am concerned that many non-insurance offerings may be preying on consumers' and companies' sense of fear and risk rather than offering any substantial risk transfer in the value they supposedly offer. And do consider this: when tapping into a fearful human state of mind, what won't somebody pay if they thought the product can make them safer? Makes marketing the product pretty easy.

Instead of looking for ways to transfer the risk and responsibility for keeping yourself safer online to someone else, return to the fundamentals of what my research found. You can often find this same psychological comfort by taking personal actions that will simply make you more cyberaware, and result in you crafting your own cybersecurity practices. Or build practices and processes around these products to enhance their effectiveness by understanding how they impact with each online style. Reducing fear is about feeling more in control of your destiny.

Often, you can either achieve this base effect for free or enhance the overall value you get from money spent on these products and services by being more selective and aware of how they work or don't work for you particularly.

For average consumers, the simple act of admitting the need to become more cyberaware is sufficient to calm you because it starts to give you an edge over the fear. In turn, this can make you a more discerning customer along the way—a good thing. And as you learn how to better protect yourself online from the most common and costly cybersecurity breaches, your stress levels fall, and the state of hypervigilance that is so punishing is gradually replaced with a feeling of being more self-determined and in control.

Basic activities and actions can help. Here are seven simple steps to take note of if you do not already do most of these today:

1. Follow all installation instructions completely for any new technology in your home, particularly making sure it is properly and securely configured. If you do not know how to do this, hire a professional!

2. Ensure that your router is NOT set to the default password and network ID before use and password protect your home and home office networks of course.

3. Make sure you subscribe to and keep up to date, antivirus and similar tools on every device and platform you own, and those attached to your network.

4. Keep your technology up to date, always loading and applying system updates and using reliable systems and vendors with proven track records of cyber safety.

5. Ensure that you do not put convenience about cybersecurity and practice safe computing including high levels of password security—not using predictable passwords, and normal rotations of your passwords which—I admit—is a pain.

6. Do not repeat the same passwords for all your systems but vary them all.

7. Consider using a password vault or similar software—reliable and recommended ones only—if this practice is not possible for you to manage on your own.

All seven steps are necessary and recommended *safe computing practices* that build a firm foundation on which to keep yourself safer online[3]. It is important to be aware of these because my test does not

---

3   For an excellent reference guide to being safe with your online technology-related practices, check out *"Cyber Smart"* by Bart McDonough (2019) published by Wiley. It is an excellent and easy to read tech guide.

replace these good tech practices, it complements them. They are not hard to implement and maintain with a modicum of effort, but without securing these basics, you invite obvious risk into your business or home that could have been avoided in the first place.

Of course, these practices only protect against *known* technical cybersecurity risks and *not* the human elements of cybersecurity as discussed. Of course, my recommendation is that you similarly address the human elements of cybersecurity risk in your home by having everyone in the household take the test! This will change the conversation inside your household, just as it does in the workplace, about how you can collectively keep yourselves all safer online as a family. Just like in chapter four, your family can adopt a cybersecurity tribe mentality too!

Whenever I do seminars, public or media appearances, I often get questions about the various consumer services targeting online safety. I always urge careful attention to the specifics of what exactly these are offering you, and at what cost, because their actual cybersecurity impact absolutely varies based on which quadrant in the test you naturally fall. That is because consumers will respond differently to different aspects of these products based on their style.

You need to firmly substantiate the value of what is being offered to you, by asking how it will impact your online behavior, and not just accept their claims of value. Will this work for me? That is the question to ask. For instance, one of the simplest and best ways to avoid becoming a victim of cybercrime is to lock down your credit—completely and entirely. This method is 100% reliable to keep you safe from anyone taking out credit in your name without you being aware. This simple act brings this risk under your direct and personal control easing fear through self-reliance. And who would you rather rely on? Yourself and your own judgment, or some paid commercial service trying to maintain its monthly revenues by preying on your fear? Perhaps you only need to be more vigilant and informed to be better off.

Fearmongering and feat-based marketing are early clues that you need to be concerned about just exactly what you are being sold. Instead, look for hopeful and more factual marketing demonstrating a connection between a tool or service and your ability to adapt it to reduce or transfer risk. Those will always be better options. And compare services and pricing among vendors and providers as well because rarely is their only one option to choose from.

Even better news about the particular services I just mentioned is that you can get free access to credit report information from all US credit agencies. By law, they must provide you with personal free access. And they must enable you to lock down your credit as well. Now early warning on both counts: these agencies do not exactly advertise this or necessarily make it easy for you to do and, when you call or e-mail, they will try and divert and deflect your efforts. Why is that when its actually often appropriate to do that as a consumer?

Because their entire business model, and all their profits, rely on sharing information they are legally entitled to collect about you with those who want to grant you credit. That's how they make money, and lots of it. By locking down your credit, you disable both cybercriminals but also legitimate credit providers you may want to have your information so you can obtain credit that would normally have paid the credit bureau to pull a credit report on you.

If you want to get more credit, you are provided with a code that, while delaying the granting of instant-on-the-spot credit only, can still facilitate legitimate companies who you want to have your information to get it within a day or so. For most consumers, the inconvenience should be entirely worth the major benefit: any theft of your personal online information becomes less valuable to criminals and less risky for you if you simply lock down your credit because they can't mess with you! Of course, you also now have an obligation to keep the code safe, protected, but still available—so responsibility calls forth again!

If you do that, while monitoring your credit report for changes, you should be more in control and know when there will be a change. Also, with so many free credit monitoring alternatives coming to the market from credit card companies, banks, and even the credit bureaus such as Equifax—who were hacked—most consumers can now get this service for free. Not much point in paying vendors for something you can get yourself for free, is there?

It is this kind of situational awareness that can aid the average consumer to become more engaged and responsible for their own cybersecurity. You cannot usually count on technology vendors to help you on this point either—in fact, as we will explore later, they are actually a part of the problem and not really offering any concrete solutions to putting you into harm's way in order to maximize their own gain. So, it becomes a balance: you want to, and maybe even need to, rely on technology for various reasons; but do so with a keen awareness of Big Tech's motives and the potential negative consequences of some of what they are offering. Take responsibility for balancing risk and reward before adopting these new technologies by considering those potential negative impacts. Compare these to the gains and absolute necessity of using this technology at this time.

This more informed and accountable approach enables you to gain control over your own information, its safety and security, and to make your personal cybersecurity profile something you accept responsibility for. In self-insuring a little bit in this way, you might even find that you are actually quite reliable and don't need to pay anyone else for help very often!

To this last point of carrying personal cybersecurity insurance—is that worth it? To answer that question more in-depth, consider the fundamental elements of insurance: the risk the insurer agrees to cover has to be modeled for claims potential and costs so the policy's premium can be appropriately priced. If it is too expensive for the coverage it provides, you will decline and self-insure and simply run the risk that the event you are trying to avoid will not occur. If that risk is minor as opposed to catastrophic, you are much more inclined not to insure against it.

If the coverage is not properly priced by the insurer, then claims overwhelm premiums and the insurance product is not profitable and is not sustainable as a product in the marketplace. At present, we are somewhere in-between with cybersecurity insurance today, and my best advice to anyone who asks me is to shop around carefully and compare coverage and costs before buying cybersecurity specific insurance. Also, check the terms of any umbrella policies you may carry because many of those will often cover cybersecurity-related claims too.

For most individuals, knowledge is power, and you need to be responsible for making these insurance decisions in this domain just as you do in many others today. But, that said, the vast majority of consumers are better off today to self-insure than they are to purchase cybersecurity insurance plans as they are currently structured and offered. Effectively, these policies do not offer the consumer much advantage because, frankly, a personal cybersecurity breach while quite awful to deal with personally, is limited to self-inflicted damage and harm to you and your family. Generally, you do not run a risk of incurring liability from another party as you might in a car accident where there are injuries or death.

That basic analysis works well for consumers. But for business, it's a very different story. Companies run the risk of extensive third-party liability from any successful attack that harms their customers or partners. With escalating cybersecurity risks and new ways to attack you coming up daily, there is no escape from the plague of time and cost that is associated with a successful cyberattack. And the rates of successful attacks are still increasing. This trend is now driving up premium rates for cyber insurance, something of great concern to every business executive that I know, and this cycle of attack and pay more is rapidly becoming unsustainable.

In 2017, the cybersecurity insurance market was a \$4B industry globally, dominated by US firms. But the market is growing fast with some researchers suggesting it will achieve \$23B in premiums by 2025.[4] You can bet, like any other cost of doing business, that much of this will be passed on to consumers and businesses in the form of higher product and service costs. Much of this premium increase will not only be new entrants into the market but also an increase in the

---

4   https://www.globenewswire.com/news-release/2019/04/10/1802202/0/
en/Cyber-Security-Insurance-Market-to-reach-23-07-Billion-by-2025-Adroit-
Market-Research.html

premium costs for those already holding cybersecurity insurance. And this statistic only covers the premium, and not the claims costs which are overwhelming insurers today and which are causing new insights into policy terms, conditions, and pricing with much of this due to the human elements of cybersecurity just discussed.

So, there are really challenging issues about how we transfer cybersecurity risk from corporations to insurers, and this market is continuing to go through metamorphoses as might be expected in what is, essentially, a constantly changing set of risk vectors to be covered.

To manage this, insurance companies must be able to discriminate risk in order to properly price policies. Pooling risk—the very premise of insurance in the first place—only works if you offer lower prices to those who take less risk and represent a lower risk of a claim from those who take more risks and represent a higher risk. But how can we assess that?

To date, that has been done using simplistic factors such as the size of the organization (representing a proxy for the costs if an attack succeeds in terms of the number of victims it likely represents); the industry in which one operates (because some industries generally hold much more valuable information than others and have business models that embed more risk than others); claims history if there is one; and, perhaps, some assessment of the robustness of a client's privacy and security practices that help avoid the most common technical breaches.

So that is all well and good IF cybersecurity was simply a technical problem. But it is not. It is a human problem, and the complexity of predicting human behavior is less obvious in a cybersecurity context than in some others. How does one insure against an unpredictable problem with a variable incidence rate and where the costs of claims are escalating rapidly?

Yet, especially mid-sized and large enterprise clients feel they cannot be without cybersecurity insurance because the potential costs of a breach and the legal consequences of being liable for the damages incurred can risk an entire company. This is a complicated problem.

In this case, an interesting analogy might be automobile insurance where we are insuring both physical damage to assets and also the liability incurred if an accident causes damages and harm to another person or their property. As a result, in most states, car insurance is mandatory so that we do not legally permit drivers to self-insure and simply assume they won't have an accident. We also have a licensing regime where you have to demonstrate the requisite skills to earn a driver's license *before* you can drive, yet everyone can simply get online risky or not. Often, we require new drivers to take a mandatory education or training class to qualify to take the driving test—again, what an interesting thought to require some level of basic technology education before, perhaps, allowing some people to be able to "drive" certain kinds of technology.

Or, an idea that has been around for some time, is that *if* one were willing to submit to some kind of pre-identification routine that validated your online identity, you would be able to participate in a *closed* internet, among only those others who had similarly been registered and validated. You would, therefore, be less inclined to commit crimes online because you would always leave a digital fingerprint. Think of it like some national online identity card scheme. While radical and not necessarily my recommendation, it is this kind of thinking about risk mitigation to *prevent it* versus *transferring the consequences and costs of an event once it happens* that is disruptive and necessary for us all to contemplate soon.

But, dialing it back more into the realm of immediately available solutions, this analogy of how we approach driving to doing business online might offer us some insights, and it might help us protect the commercial future of the internet which, because of high rates of cybercrime and fraud, is rapidly becoming unstable and unsustainable in some instances.

As outlandish as some of this may seem now, if we cannot arrest the rate of successful attacks plaguing the internet, we may eventually arrive at a point where, for the simple certainty of making sure that everyone is protected, we may mandate anyone operating commercially in cyberspace to hold basic cybersecurity insurance. That might remain our only choice if the internet remains so crime-infested globally.

What about requiring that someone in the organization hold a "license" (of analogous credential) to prove the knowledge necessary to safely operate interconnected technology in the open internet before letting them operate commercially online? This need could arise simply because as the certainty of being successfully attacked increases, consumers must be permitted to easily hold companies liable for damages without having to resort to court battles. The cards are simply too much in favor of the companies, and the little guy will always lose and end up holding the bag for the sins of Big Tech again. So, without mandatory insurance coverage as a backstop, the entire commercial value of the internet will eventually become overwhelmed by the growing costs and hassles of claims related to cybersecurity risk and damage done to innocent consumers.

If requiring licenses and insurance to operate online is adopted in the future, it will require substantial participation by the government to ensure it is affordable to obtain and to create a legal regime that would essentially make cybersecurity insurance rates regulated and subject to review. Otherwise, insurers will become profiteers as a result of the imposition of this insurance requirement and that is not fair.

Immediately some will argue that the mere involvement of government as regulator makes this an unwieldy and unworkable solution. There is ample truth to that. But, in worse news still for this model, it may even be in higher-risk industries that attract constant attack that only insurance underwritten by government will actually be economically feasible to ensure tolerable premiums are available to some commercial participants in high-risk sectors of the economy.

In another model, again in a similar way to how we approach auto insurance today, we might start by offering a discount to companies that can *prove* they are less of a risk while still leaving the question of coverage as voluntary but recommended. Using this approach, as one measures claims experience, organizations participate in partially setting their own rates by actively mitigating cybersecurity risks more actively just like the "name your own price tools" advertised for safe drivers by some auto insurers. This approach would increase the likelihood that companies would take the investments required of them to stay safer online more seriously because there would be an offsetting benefit by reducing their required cybersecurity insurance premiums. Of course, this only works if carrying cybersecurity insurance is mandated. Otherwise, with rising premiums, companies will simply drop coverage instead.

While some of the early thinking in this chapter may seem outlandish on so many levels, I think we are experiencing an alarming acceleration of compromise to so many of our largest and most capable Big Tech companies that any assurance that these will stop anytime soon is suspect. But it must stop because the costs of compliance are unsustainable in the longer-term, creating a problem that could start to impair the value of even doing business online.

Consequently, we are going to have to think about more than simply improving cybersecurity; perhaps we are going to have to start to adopt models where it is simply built in to the price of admission to adopting and using technology. That could involve some of the techniques I have outlined in this book or a whole host of other initiatives and activities in the business world that also demonstrate a positive impact on keeping us all safer online.

But it mostly starts only if we can somehow model cybersecurity risk and mitigating tactics more actively. Then we can address fundamentally changing the ways we approach cybersecurity insurance and become more able to differentiate true cybersecurity risk down to the individual company, employee, and/or consumer level. That is the breakthrough my test offers us: a way to *differentiate* risk and *discriminate* interventions by aligning them to our individual personality, so they work better than existing generic solutions to this complex problem. To date, this has measurably reduced total cybersecurity risk by sensitizing folks to the ways their own behavior can contribute to making them less safe when online.

So, before we are forced to consider those more draconian approaches to the mandatory licensing, isolated networks, or requiring insurance against these risks, let's make sure that each and every consumer and company has done everything they can to become more cyberaware and accountable first. Maybe that can move the needle of cybersecurity risk in our collective favor.

CHAPTER SIX:

UNDER ATTACK FROM WITHIN

Of any nation in the world, the United States of America is a beacon of democracy whose history is firmly rooted in a constitution framed by the Founding Fathers enshrining inviolable rights to all citizens. This legacy is both a foundational blessing and a growing curse in the interconnected digital age in which we now live and where easy radicalization of those looking for a cause often leads to great harm. Again, this is not a new problem so much as it is an existing problem where hate is growing to scale at the same rate as technology spreads.

Increasing rates of domestic terrorism, often cyber-inspired, are causing pain not only in America but around the world. While Americans often see themselves as global peacemakers and dedicated defenders of democracy, the USA has lots of global enemies who disagree, and the internet gives these foreign enemies new tools to spread propaganda and hate. And they relish doing that. So, this is both a domestic and an international existential threat.

For honest citizens, an awful conclusion arises from the rapid rise in internet-inspired terrorism: a fear that it is now fellow citizens turning their ire and guns on other innocent citizens that is the real problem. The conclusion? We are being attacked from within and it's dangerous.

I have spent years studying the law of armed conflict and specifically comparative national security law globally, a topic on which I often write. This is a long-standing body of established law, and in the case of regulating war, this legal history dates back two centuries. These were painstaking multilateral efforts among nations when war was understood to be both inevitable, and perhaps even on occasion beneficial, but something which still required the rule of law to govern in critical respects, although I admit to abhorrence at the intent to govern something this damaging. Of course, the basis for all law was the principal idea that war occurred among nations and in situ, often requiring us to go and fight wars someplace else and not in the homeland.

However, the technology of armed conflict has rapidly evolved as the defense industry has innovated technically, especially in the last half of the last century. Even more intriguing is the spectacular rise of the internet which has resulted in digital weapons being deployed in cyberspace by various countries, rapidly transforming the idea of war as we knew it in the past into cyberwar as we have come to know it in the present and future.

It is interesting to think about what it means when a computer virus can be delivered by our enemy straight into the operating systems of our electrical grid or dams for instance, and that this could cause death and destruction that involves no part of traditional war involving troops, weapons, and battlefields. So, cyberwar can cause kinetic damage, up to and including death. Remembering the very objective of war is death, disruption, and destruction, the weaponization of the internet is rapidly proving to be a great warfare advance. And it is especially effective at information warfare and social disruption, another major objective in any war.

Having written about this strategic, legal and moral phenomenon elsewhere, I will not repeat that here except for one aspect of this important debate that deserves inclusion. That is the perceptual connection between any kind of tool that may be associated with "profiling" anyone in some respect, and either breaking the law or fearing a deep state conspiracy by our government to control us and deprive us of our freedoms. Profiling often gets a bad rap. When it is used to ensure that we keep all citizens collectively safe in a rapidly evolving online threat landscape, it becomes a vital tool that is treated very differently in the United States than elsewhere, potentially putting us at a strategic disadvantage as a nation.

This situation derives from our constitutional framework, which offers extraordinarily strong protections to citizens from abuse of their rights. Inherent in this assumption is that threats are more likely to come from outside the country, rather than from those same protected citizens. Therefore, we enact all kinds of laws—and particularly the Patriot Act for instance—designed to assist law enforcement in the rapid detection, profiling, tracking, and eventual apprehension of those engaged in any act of internationally connected or sponsored terrorism. And pre-9/11, the majority of cases the FBI and other agencies are tracking to prevent harm to the homeland were internationally inspired or connected. Post 9/11, once harm intruded into the Homeland, this resulted in a declaration of "War on Terrorism" and a deliberate, targeted effort among Western allies to defeat terrorist evils around the world.

This particularly American view, generally shared across North America, insists that the primary threat is outside our country and acts of terrorism are inspired by devotion to a foreign land, cause, or religion. This was essential logic in how the war on terrorism was first executed.

It also resulted in a base instinct that provokes instant accusations that any domestic profiling tool, especially in the wrong hands, is simply inappropriate and misguided by definition. We cannot turn that scrutiny onto citizens because they are obviously not the problem: outsiders are. Culturally, this is often linked to our fear about the presence of some sort of "deep state" within the US government and, if left to itself, it would naturally deny us our personal privacy rights, eventually controlling all of society. Or inviting the illuminati in![5]

This culturally autonomic response to testing and profiling of citizens—just as it is with the fight-or-flight response itself—suggests an absolute denial of a new truth. Of late, the existential threat faced by Americans is as much from within the US in the form of domestic terrorism (DT) as it is from any foreign-backed source. And if you talk in any detail to law enforcement agencies engaged in this fight, they will tell you that examples of international terrorism (IT) are falling, while incidents sparked by internal radicals with no connection to any organization or country outside the US, are now the primary threat. Aren't the consequences the same so why even distinguish them[6]—they are simply intentional acts of terrorism, period.

So, we hamper the use of tools that have been proven effective at fighting international threats while denying those same tools—and an associated speed of response to avert tragic consequences—to heroes fighting this battle on our behalf inside this country. This arises because of a perceived conflict between our national security, privacy, and constitutional rights.

In exploring this issue, we must understand by whom and when the Constitution was framed. As a student of the law, I was made deeply aware of the legal tradition of originalism demanding respect for the Framers' constitutional intentions. This view supports complete legal primacy of the Constitution, preserving its stability and demands literal respect for this founding document. There is validity to this position legally and morally, and it should not be dismissed out-of-hand. This is also the primary argument often advanced for why we differentiate between "American persons" in criminal law (mostly citizens and lawful permanent residents) and those who are not because they are not

---

5   For a great example of debunking popular online conspiracy theories, visit https://www.vox.com/2015/5/19/8624675/what-is-the-real-illuminati for a discussion about the historical roots of the Illuminati and why they persist as an internet hoax today.
6   See this very thought-provoking opinion piece from two law enforcement agents on this very point: https://www.nytimes.com/2019/09/11/opinion/nypd-domestic-terrorism.html

entitled to these same constitutional protections.

Yet, the Framers themselves were intent on creating an independent country that would follow a very different path on questions of civil liberties from the dominant European monarchies of their day. In its entirety, the founding premise was to offer each and every individual the promise of "life, liberty and the pursuit of happiness" as expressed in the 1776 Declaration of Independence. Although separate documents, these are contemporaneous and connected in spirit at the birth of America. Freedom underpins both documents and, in originalist terms, is a core value to protect at all costs. If one accepts this position, then anything that impairs freedom unconstitutionally risks the entire premise of our democracy.

Globally speaking, this promise is not available in many countries; even those politically goaded into increased democracy by the United States ironically. There is ample evidence of eroding rights in many places and increasing political strife too. And many authors have previously dwelt on the vexing matter of comparing various kinds of political, religious, and economic systems of organizing nations found around the globe. So, I will not.

But therein lies the dilemma that makes me thoughtfully resist originalism on an important point: the internet, obviously not even possible to have conceived of when the Constitution was framed, has inherent qualities that risk unhinging the promise of America if we are careless in our contemporary interpretation of the Constitution. And we cannot deny this.

The internet is a fever swamp of malcontent, mistruths, and fake conspiracy theories that are unregulated and easily persuasive to those seeking a cause—for better or for worse. The internet grants an incredible ability to easily and deliberately amplify evil and radicalize those vulnerable to persuasion. This includes obvious targets, particularly those with sociopathic tendencies or mental health issues for example. But also, the politically or economically disenfranchised or disadvantaged who quickly become socially marginalized and easy prey for those offering a way to express their growing angst and anger.

This is a grave crisis and growing threat to our national security. The internet has essentially become a weapon of *mass information destruction,* literally impairing the ability of many individual Americans to enjoy life, liberty, and the pursuit of happiness. Ironically, this is the very ideal advanced at this nation's birth. Yet, free speech protections are now being used by those with criminal intent to justify evil, harmful, and even ultimately fatal attacks on fellow citizens that originated online. These actions were never imagined as possible by those who framed the Constitution—it presumed citizen loyalty and patriotism as a base assumption.

Nor could they have foreseen the ability of foreign powers to influence our internal political affairs from afar using remotely controlled technology to sow domestic mistrust and discontent as they so easily do today. Foreign interference in domestic affairs is never okay.

So even originalists must now ask how we plan to maintain important constitutional protections while dealing with a modern technology phenomenon which seems to threaten these very same rights. According to the FBI, rates of domestic terrorist incidents across the nation now exceed a rate of one per day, a frightening escalation. The scope of the attacks is also creating more mass casualties, and many Americans report a fear that no public place is actually safe today from the threat of gun violence anymore. This dilemma should make us mindful—regardless of political affiliation—of considering how we balance individual liberty and freedom while protecting collective national security, because we need to make America safe again.

Elaborating, we must address the increasing incidence of terrorism globally that is particularly fueled by race and nationalism. This plague is not just found in the United States but is also a trend seen in other Western countries like Canada, the UK, and France, for example. These growing nationalist movements are a threat to global civility and peace to be feared.

While there are at least three credible definitions of crimes related to domestic terrorism at the federal level, associated data sources and crime statistics provided by the likes of the FBI all confirm this fact:

there is a rising rate of incidence of these types of crimes regardless of the specifics of the legal nuances involved. And much of this has to do with white nationalism.

So, we must avoid absorbing esoteric legal arguments and nuances and demand that politicians and legislatures worldwide do what they can to address the root causes of these acts—and that is not just about lax gun control in the US although that is a definite contributing factor.

Instead, that is ultimately about *information literacy* and the ongoing abuse of social media to weaponize false information. Disinformation campaigns – all well documented by law enforcement – are being actively used to recruit disaffected youth in particular. The presence of platforms—such as 8chan or Gab for instance—solely designed under the guise of freedom of speech to actually perpetuate terrorism, white nationalist conspiracies or to legitimize racism is a significant social plague. There must be no doubt that internet-inspired and promoted domestic terrorism is a crisis, and the corruption of online technology platforms designed for free information exchange into radicalizing platforms for evil is the real crime, and something we should expect Big Tech to rally against even if it's complicated or costly. We must act authoritatively and decisively to not extend free speech protections to those promoting hatred and violence and we need legislators to address this in law, and fast.

The awful results of inaction on this point are obvious: once unleashed this threat does not discriminate and harms and kills citizens simply pursuing their life, liberty, and individual pursuit of happiness, whether or not undertaken by foreign-born or US-born perpetrators. Just ask the victims of the Tsarnaev brothers who were the architects of the 2013 Boston Marathon bombing—innocently attending an annual sporting event always considered safe and fun for families. Or consider the fourteen murdered and twenty-two injured in the 2015 San Bernardino attacks, a city many thought until then was a safe place to live peaceful lives.

Each of these gruesome attacks—all well documented by the media—had an internet-related component. It involved recruiting, training, and managing these attackers from afar before they unleashed their deadly fury. These were early and classic examples of international terrorism because their nexus was to a foreign country or organization.

None of these acts were undertaken by visitors to the US, as once would have been required to execute a terrorist attack on our shores. Rather, our enemies now attack us *from within*—fellow citizens and residents who are on "remote-control" through the internet. Because the worldwide web reaches across national boundaries without regard to borders, morality, or rule of law, it makes it easier than ever to recruit those among us who would disrupt and destroy our country and its way of life. This has frightening implications, but again fear is not the right response. Rather, I would suggest activism arising from an understanding of the root cause of this and thoughtful national reflection about how to respond makes more sense.

Now consider a different kind of recent attack: the mass shooting that happened in El Paso just as this book was going to print, frightfully one of two back-to-back mass shootings in a single, sad weekend. It involved unsuspecting innocents shopping at a local Wal-Mart whose lives were cruelly snuffed out in an instant. Over twenty-two dead and many more injured. Predictably this will not be the last attack of its kind any time soon for this has become a wretched national plague of daunting scope and scale in America right now.

And what do we know of the killer's motive in that attack? Mostly just an online "manifesto," more akin to a racist and xenophobic screed, that inspired an attack on fellow citizens. He was angry about an "invasion" of the immigrants into the US, in his mind stealing jobs and ruining his birthright entitlement to live in a white homeland. Of note, these are common but dangerously incendiary messages in the political discourse of our nation presently. And the investigation revealed the stark nature of how the perpetrator's fears and biases, in this case, were stoked online by the 8chan platform—a really radical and racist online forum long known by law enforcement to be filled with hate speech. Yet it remains online still, continuing to stoke evil inside our next mass shooter.

Regrettably, this is exactly the kind of site found so easily all over the internet. And under current laws, it is not easily eradicated, controlled, or dismantled because of strong protections offered under US freedom of expression laws. Most current laws do not readily apply to this type of online forum even, further tying law enforcements' hands as they idly watch hate spew and anger foment online ultimately leading to mass shootings that kill innocent citizens.

What should shock any reader is that children and young adults easily find these sites, become enchanted by finding validation for their discontent, becoming socially isolated and eventually radicalized more easily than most of us imagine. Youth especially become easy targets for manipulation, both from abroad or here at home. The difference now is that those terrorists, once radicalized and recruited online, become internal threats against soft targets all across the country, creating a home-grown network of domestic terrorists willing to kill us in public places based on the validation they receive for their views online. This is pure evil.

I believe the Framers assumed, apart from normal criminal behavior, that most citizens of the United States would share by birthright and assimilation the tenets of this democracy that make it what it is. Sharing, instructing, and reinforcing those rights is celebrated as patriotic. It was unthinkable to transgress these rights and attack the nation in the name of other religions, crowns, countries, or organizations. But that essence has dramatically changed.

I am so certain of this because of the very nature of the founding of America. At birth, it sought independence from a foreign country and crown that its citizens could no longer abide. It yearned for freedom, eventually enshrining that as a founding principle. That deeply embedded birthright as a nation assumed a commonality of experience to create a pluralism of commitment to the ideals of nationhood itself. But is that any longer the case when American citizens are prepared to become terrorists against their neighbors after being radicalized online? Just what exactly is the proper, but still balanced, response to that phenomenon when it now kills hundreds of innocent Americans every year? That absolutely demands we find solutions to this frightful problem and restore hope, making upcoming elections a powerful opportunity for change by demanding all politicians join with the people to forge solutions to fix this. I am personally astonished that growing public anger about this issue has not unleashed action by legislators.

When such potential evil lurks in online platforms, finding the right societal response to protect ourselves from harm is a pressing matter. How do we balance individual rights to privacy and freedom of expression with a legitimate need to detect and prevent an increasing rate of domestic terrorism? To what extent do we start to hold Big Tech accountable for the consequences and liability that its products enable? It is incomprehensible to me that in any other realm where a manufacturer turned out a flawed product—in this instance, one in which the use of the product leads to the death of innocent victims—that there is almost no legal hope to hold them accountable. Why? Because Big Tech resists any notion they are "publishers" and thus should be accountable for what users express online on their platforms.

Instead, they hold to a pattern of avoiding negligence by entirely putting the blame for what is said and done on the user, keeping themselves immune from consequence. Now we have seen a shifting trend in this regard, not born of a sudden acceptance of responsibility by Big Tech for its actions though. Instead, once again, to try and limit the scope of government regulators and their desire to force a day of reckoning with Big Tech.

If you want to be truly scared about the extent of this problem in real-time, visit this site to see a list of terrorism investigations currently underway. (https://www.fbi.gov/investigate/terrorism). See how many incidents, just this month, were either detected, foiled, or prosecuted. It should cause shock and awe in any reader.

Then consider the extent to which online media—of any sort—is a feature of the crimes recorded there. How can any informed citizen deny we have an urgent problem? We may, in fact, have an epic battle brewing—this time between Big Tech's profit machine and holding them responsible for what is published on their sites when it inspires violence and terrorism. There is a causal effect—what the law defines as a tort—and although we are not there yet, we may be on the cusp of it soon. And I hope public dialogue about this will be sparked accordingly.

However, if we stridently overhype this particular aspect of the internet, we also risk growing fearful—the very thing this book is trying to help mitigate. So instead, I want us to become emboldened as a public, demanding proper legal responsibility from Big Tech to admit they shoulder some, but not all, of the blame for this mess. It is their products and platforms that are being used to create this mess, so we should force some of their billions in profits out of their hands and make them directly deploy it to help solve the problem, right?

Similarly, while we may prefer to deny Russian meddling in our elections for any host of reasons valid or otherwise, it is a fact that they are interfering in our online national political debate—and quite effectively of late. They will also continue to do so, for they are our foresworn enemy from long ago and this too is not new news, or fake news! This is not about hacking into voting systems by the way—that is way too obvious a game to pursue that is easily detected and eventually protected against. Rather, we are talking about efforts to *hack the human mind*. This is ultimately one of the biggest threats to our democracy actually—affecting it one person at a time.

The Russians have for years invested in and used disinformation campaigns to achieve political objectives both domestically and abroad. They are not an ally and must never be treated as one. They will never accept us as anything other than a rival and foe to their ascendancy to political influence and global dominance all in their own interest.

Therefore, they will do anything they can and again from afar, to influence us if it helps them achieve their political aims. This means they have a natural interest in the outcome of our democratic electoral process as it relates to their own self-interest. Naturally, the internet presents itself as an incredible tool that is highly effective in the pursuit of that goal, displacing spying and recruiting of local communists as allies because, quite simply, that doesn't work very well comparatively. But online disinformation campaigns do. Striving to resemble legitimate sites by posing as news sources, political groups and such makes their detection among the naïve or badly intentioned unlikely, and their resulting impact that much higher.

Across the nation, we have declining rates of overall information literacy generally. Many Americans cannot adequately assess what they read online, its veracity, truthfulness, or underlying intention to manipulate. And all the current rhetoric about "fake news" doesn't help. This climate makes it easy to interfere when, generally speaking in polls of late, more than 50% of citizens simply accept what they read online as being true. That makes protecting our democracy among and for ourselves that much harder to accomplish but an absolutely essential 21st century challenge.

But scant substantive debate is actually occurring in the public discourse about this. Instead, the fact base we hear debated in the media and among politicians is another false narrative: that truth is relative. It is not the case. And the consequences of eroding this belief are being denied in many quarters ("fake news" and "alternative facts") as information becomes weaponized as a tool to foster divisive politics and stoke social unrest.

Truthfully, this is not a story of Left and Right, because neither party is blameless in using these techniques to their political advantage. This phenomenon is consuming our democracy and enabling powerful false online influences to promote hatred, incite acts of domestic terrorism, and stoke racial tensions to disrupt the social progress of our nation. It is also going to make us weak and expose us to more attacks, a disappointing outcome.

So how does this relate to my tool? Well, it turns out that the likelihood of falling prey to false information online is linked to the degree to which you tolerate the risk of propagating false information by not checking it sources. The other axis provides insight into the extent to which you will learn, accept, and apply simple rules about the integrity of information sources before relying on them as truth, sharing, or endorsing them online. These are important first steps in preventing the propagation of false memes and narratives online.

While I have not yet researched this sufficiently to more complete-ly understand it, there is something inherent that speaks to each of our own unique responsibilities to help quell the spread of false informa-tion online. As a society, we must stop naively promoting it and ignor-ing the impact false information has on eroding trust and truth among us over time. This seems to be another area where more self-awareness of our instinctive online behavior can be helpful, and I will continue to explore this intriguing research question in the future.

Meantime, what should be clear is the need to equip our intelligence agencies, law enforcement, and the military with every possible tool, method, and access point we can to locate, validate, and pursue appro-priate actions, both here and abroad, to root out the evils of domestic terrorism by apprehending those responsible for its propagation. To do so more effectively, we need to engage in a civil and thoughtful de-bate about the trade-offs we are willing to accept as citizens that may impinge gently on personal liberty to secure more collective national security. The time to undertake that debate is sooner rather than later.

At this point, any even limited action is better than inaction on something so threatening to the homeland. Often, after disclosures such as the Snowden affair, we witness an often instinctive, knee-jerk reaction to what we perceive as frightening disclosures about this problem. Deep in the DNA of the nation is a mistrust of govern-ment, and this leads us to conclude that too much power accrues to them rather than us, and so we rebalance to individual liberty as the gold standard. This may prevent us all cogitating on a complex issue more thoughtfully, and to more fully delving into the potentially dev-astating consequences of this response if it is not more considered of the technology risks the internet brings to our shores. This is a vitally important future issue for all citizens, and most certainly not just our politicians, to wrestle with and to resolve in our own best interests to help keep our nation safe.

Similarly, we must exorcise politics from the debate about not only Russian interference in our elections, but also about improving citizens' understanding of information literacy and starting from a very young age. We must become deliberate in preventing online manipulation of information that is easily prevented with only a modicum of education about how to detect it. Otherwise, we are not protecting core American ideals because the political debates we engage in are falsely promulgated and inflamed to the advantage of our foreign adversaries. The conclusion we must come to as a nation is that whenever the internet is used to sow false information to us, its acceptance only supports domestic mistrust among us.

Permitting this to continue enables them—whoever the "them" happens to be in the moment even if that actually turns out to be "us" ultimately—to prevail over our democracy. This is an exactly what the founding fathers did not intend to occur. Instead, we must interfere with our enemies' ability to promote their manipulative messages online spreading fear into our political system. We must replace this with legitimate online debate about domestic issues of real concern to real citizens instead. Don't accept the stoking of false memes planted by foreign interests all designed to spark paralyzing political divisiveness that weakens us all[7].

Being naïve to this reality borders on treason I suggest, a word that should be used sparingly and only when it is truly applicable given it potency. Yet, the current state of affairs violates the very spirit of protecting a country that claims to be about life, liberty, and the pursuit of happiness instead risks becoming a model of murder, suicide, subjugation, and the pursuit of demeaning others. It is high time for us to put aside our political differences—which I note are in large part what is being exploited by those trying to harm us—and to act together to re-inspire hope and displace the fear that radicalization is imposing globally. The internet has become a mean place because it so often provokes the worst in us as we disconnect ourselves from social accountability by saying things we would not say to each other

---

7   For more insight into this trend, visit the Global Disinformation Index at disinformationindex.org

in person, breaking long-established social norms. It cannot continue without causing abject harm to many.

Maybe the time has finally arrived for us to consider promoting more civility online, such as calling out the bullies, deflecting mistruths, and avoiding surrender to the worst of our human instincts. This could recapture a sense of humanity and empathy for others online as a defined feature of normal digital engagement—to collectively redefine online social expectations if you like. If we combine that expressed intention to be more respectful online with teaching our children how to be more information literate, we reject hate and false division.

Perhaps it is also not too late for younger generations to escape the obvious digital narcissism that is such a feature of online tropes today, including from the very top of political leadership in this country. That disappointing role modelling is not helping fix this problem, but it is what we seem willing to tolerate still. So, perhaps in the coming years, a shift in thinking will create an opportunity for Americans to become purveyors of online hope instead of online hate. And that could really make America great again, don't you think?

CHAPTER SEVEN:
GETTING NAKED ONLINE

It seems superficially clear society is inclining toward total transparency no matter the social implications. At least it seems so based on the sheer volume of how much personal information about the most intimate and mundane details of their lives many share online. Further, we have seen the rise of questionable organizations, such as WikiLeaks, laying claim to forcing transparency by "shining light into the darkness of government and corporate operations" but who essentially induce those with access to steal top-secret information to share online regardless of the human costs. But this version of social transparency ignores accompanying dangers of untested online transparency often creating untold or unknown risks for so many.

Considering that humans are social creatures who substantially follow stricter social hierarchies than we like to admit, tribalism of old has simply been replaced by newer social constructs and strata that involve race, religion, politics, economic status, professional profiles, work affiliations, and the like. Often social apparatus—and most especially the internet and social media platforms of all sorts today—can be used to enhance or even manipulate our social standing and to establish an untested social profile. This often leads to a constant state of over-sharing: putting up the mundane details of our daily existence to share with our "friends," seeking likes and reposting as if that were a social scorecard, and wanting to ensure our relevance by a mounting online social presence even among strangers.

Meanwhile, there is considerable evidence uncovered by researchers of a declining engagement in what might be referred to as "legitimate or traditional social activity"—that which involves leveraging in-person social connection and deepening intimacy in a romantic relationship or friendship for example. The need to affiliate—to belong—and to feel validated by making and keeping these connections is deeply embedded in our human social constructs.

So what contribution does this new level of supposed online connection and community contribute to satisfying those basic human needs? While the jury is still out on final conclusions, it is arguably much less satisfying than what has been promised to us by Big Tech. It does not seem as if technology-intermediated social connections have the same impact as those we do in person, and any notion of replacing one with the other as equally impactful is actually socially dangerous, for it can often leave us more vulnerable to exploitation.

Why? Because most of us are *not naked online*. I do **not** mean this in the literal sense of appearing naked online, although that too is a constant feature of the internet where pornography continues to be one of the most profitable online businesses ever. Given human nature, that is not surprising and is of little importance to this chapter actually even though the connection between technology and sexuality is intriguing as a topic, I will leave it to others.

Rather, even as we lie online about and to ourselves, we place extraordinary trust in others online not to do the same thing. This is perverse in so many respects. And we engage in social behaviors online that we absolutely would not do in person because they break social codes, suggesting a sort of negative online "halo effect," where getting behind the computer keyboard separates us from traditional and long-standing standards of social conduct. This *dissociative effect* may be a substantial contributor to our declining online behavior and may be a further factor worthy of exploration to define its social impact both on and offline.

For example, surveys show that most people under the age of thirty have exchanged either a nearly naked or entirely naked picture of themselves online *with a virtual stranger* at some point. This is completely a function of the internet. We have also developed an entire lexicon to describe this behavior such as "dick pics" and "tit to toe shots" and so on, suggesting this as a common social behavior online. Culturally, this breaks down connections between sexuality and intimate connection. For instance, can you imagine meeting a stranger in a bar for a few minutes, not knowing much about them but being attracted to them, and then hiking your shirt or dropping your drawers to seal the deal? You would immediately be arrested for public nudity, flashing, or a similar misdemeanor in most jurisdictions!

It is important not to overstate some of what is emerging online as being *more deviant* simply because it's *more visible* to us. That would be a mistake. For instance, do any readers remember what might have happened in wood-paneled basements of old? Or at drive-ins when they were popular? Perhaps some drinking, fumbling in the dark and fooling around? I'll bet most of you can remember games like spin the bottle, too, and truth or dare. Of course, some of you may never have done any of this, and some were reluctant participants, but some jumped right in and lead the game's start! That fits with my model.

By definition, and particularly through adolescence, we are all driven to experiment and discover our fundamental selves by separating from parental control and beginning to exercise autonomous decision-making that is shaped by our underlying values, our experiences, and our upbringing to date. Human nature ensures this includes elements of our emerging sexual identity, orientation, and erotic interests as uncomfortable as that makes parents. This is normal.

In the internet-enabled world of today, instead of this being less visible and perhaps hidden in a downstairs basement, at a tent in a campground, in the woods, or the back seat of a car parked somewhere private, now it occurs online in real-time. But two kids of the same age exchanging nude pictures is just a modern expression of an age-old behavior and not child pornography per se, although in some jurisdictions lapses in prosecutorial judgment have triggered exactly this kind of legal overreach. That victimizes youthful indiscretion using criminal codes designed to target adult pedophiles exploiting children, which truly is deviant behavior that must be arrested. This means we may all need to reflect a bit, perhaps settle down socially, and collectively adopt a better understanding of just exactly what these behaviors represent and whether or not they are criminal and creepy in origin, or simply an updated version of normal behavior in a modern context.

While I understand the anxious parent who says—rightly—that the stakes of doing this online seem so much more devastating because actions taken online when we are young now remain visible forever as youngsters live out their lives online, often without restraint. You bet they truly are getting naked online. However, this must be contextualized over time by society because, as it becomes normal for this to occur and everyone is doing it, our understanding of it being deviant is reduced and replaced with a sense of normal social proportions that reduces our sense of shock because the event itself is no longer socially shocking. That is what I mean when I say society is having a tough time keeping up with the pace of technology change in terms of fully absorbing the implications of social media. But it does eventually catch up, and some adult fears may simply be overwrought parenting.

Regardless, we need not belabor the point too much: simply put, there is lots and lots of nudity, pornography, and other difficult stuff online, much of which is quite horrifying. But this has always been part of a darker underbelly of a prurient society through history. Some of it is *not* what we think it is though, and we simply need to catch up socially to new ways of doing the most normal of human things. But the fact that these deviant, and especially criminal behavioral elements of society are conducted more easily online—perhaps even accentuated—should be of no particular surprise to any reader. It simply calls on us to enforce existing laws where those are broken—an enforcement issue—or adjusting our social mores as we seem to be doing to integrate new behaviors that emerge online within or around existing social codes of conduct.

But that is also not entirely the point of this provocatively titled chapter either. Instead, I am talking about how we as a society strip away the false transparency found online currently and replace it with more accountability to properly be transparent online. How do we move from a place of simply trusting something—a news source, someone's identity or intentions, or a new app—and instead, replace that initial online trust with a natural and sustained state of *skepticism*. Because we should be skeptical of much of what can be found online.

Now that is significantly different from fear, and that is an essential nuance of this chapter. Some level of natural skepticism is both required, natural, and quite sustainable without incurring the exhaustion hypervigilance triggers. The mere fact that so much of what is online is actually either false, deliberately provocative, or outright manipulative, could leave us grasping for the truth and embarrassed when we fall prey and are discovered as easy rubes who were exploited for someone's social ingenuity unless we can develop a healthy sense of skepticism when we need it. "Why didn't I spot that little hint before I clicked on that ransomware link?" is a question you may have to ask yourself otherwise someday soon. Consider the recent examples of the costs being inflicted on municipalities across America today. In a coordinated attack, criminals targeted city employees inducing them to click on a ransomware link that would then infect city systems holding an entire city or town hostage. The example I am personally most familiar with because it directly impacted me was in Baltimore, Maryland, in June 2019. A single employee simply trusted the wrong person online at the wrong time and place. That one click infected the entire city's systems with ransomware, tying it up for weeks at tremendous cost and inconvenience! Since then this has now happened to hundreds of municipalities everywhere[8].

This returns us squarely to what the CyberIQ test profiles reveal: all of us are more or less transparent by nature and more or less trusting. And some folks online are willing to exploit that for their own purposes, criminal or otherwise. This fact makes each of us vulnerable in different degrees to different kinds of positive and negative social consequences online: from being overly trusting and vulnerable to being overly skeptical and risking social anxiety, isolation, and loneliness. Those are real human consequences of new online technologies.

Although my test does not specifically address these two traits themselves, they do turn out to be derivatives of your innate perception of risk-reward-rule trade-offs anyway.

That is because, to be skeptical, both our experience and our innate nature are combined to produce results that help us understand triggers of when, where, and why we should be skeptical to protect ourselves. For the reasons already outlined so far, a state of hypervigilance induced by fear makes us overly skeptical all the time and trying to sense the source of danger from fear that may arise. As exhaustion settles in, and our defenses fall, so does our level of vigilance which plays right into the hands of third parties trying to exploit us for their own gain.

Ironically, by moving our own daily habits toward greater online transparency—validating sources, confirming identity, not oversharing and protecting ourselves from social manipulations—we have the potential to move the entire online needle on this scale one individual at a time. As each individual becomes more transparent and more demanding of transparency from others, the overall online climate will become more transparent.

As we make it more transparent through sustained individual ef-

---

8   See https://www.houstonchronicle.com/news/politics/texas/article/ Hackers-cripple-22-Texas-government-agencies-14365280.php for an excellent summary of these types of attacks on municipal governments.

fort, we have a collective effect of making it harder for those who loathe transparency and exploit anonymity to hide and function freely. They become more visible and suspicious more immediately, and their behavior becomes a detectable aberration that highlights their false motives and intent. This is crucial and can help reduce online crime, fraud and hacks.

But eradicating crime across society is hard and will never be entirely achieved, including online. That is because some among us will always show criminal intent and exhibit deviant, sociopathic, or psychotic tendencies. This is often what drives them to crime in the first place.

And the standardized cyberIQtest discussed in this book will absolutely **not** detect or protect you from those intentionally out to harm you. It does not profile for criminal intent. You must learn to detect and avoid this as best you can on your own. And there are a plethora of tests, and using criminal background checks for example, that can help accomplish exactly that today.

But skepticism as a well-honed skill **can** help protect you from criminal intent making it a worthwhile addition to your online personal cybersecurity arsenal. By developing that instinct—and avoiding ascribing false transparency to what you see online, it can protect you and your family from that dangerous point of first contact. Skepticism protects you from falsely trusting online when that is not warranted and can help you spot those with false and manipulative online intent sooner and more easily. A good thing for you but not for the online bad guys!

CHAPTER EIGHT:

IMPROVING CYBERSECURITY AWARENESS

Writing this book during a scorching hot mid-Atlantic summer, the first heatwave of the season had just arrived. The weather fore-casters were cackling with warnings about those most vulnerable to heatstroke and exhaustion: the young and the elderly. Apt, I thought.

It turns out those most prone to online manipulation are these same two groups, but for different reasons worth exploring and comparing from insights in the previous chapter. That applied more to working adults, but we can apply those same concepts to help those we love who are older or younger to develop a healthy and appropriate sense of online skepticism too.

Turns out that while their instincts can vary for some addition-al demographic or illness-related reasons, the base conclusions about how to actually impact the online behavior of the younger and older members of our society follow the same patterns as for younger and middle-aged working adults. This is no surprise given a common hu-man nature.

Among our youngest members of society, now digital natives who have grown up always knowing the internet, there is a naivety about their trust in the online world that is eventually replaced through experience, sometimes hard-won. Like everything else, with age apparently comes wisdom, or so we assume.

Yet where their inherent personality traits lead them when they lack experience is where the real trouble starts. As they grow up, their constant digital experiences will begin to overwhelm other experiences at home, at school, and in the world confirming their mistrust of the real world and replacing it slowly with a preference for the artifice and comfort of their artificially constructed online world. There can even be mild dissociative inclinations where they mentally depart from reality, a dangerous precondition to psychopathy which we must monitor for and contain before it creates harm to them and others.

For most, early online activity will eventually compel or propel them to actions, activities, and places online where they should not be found. That is the primary risk for parents to be aware of, and I have much more to say on this to follow, but not to feed fear. Instead I think there is much insight that can help assuage your fear, and understand how youth behave online.

Meanwhile, seniors and more elderly members of our extended families are not digital natives by any stretch and, generally speaking, they have been trying vainly for years to simply keep up with the progress of technology sufficiently to not feel isolated, inept, and left out.

Whatever their motive for participating online ("my grandchildren are more accessible to me on Facebook than in person"), they are doing so often vastly under-equipped with the instincts necessary to protect themselves from being exploited. The single largest group of online cybersecurity attacks are against people living alone aged sixty-five or older, simply because they are so vulnerable online[9]. And so often with

---

9   For an excellent summary of both the facts and insights related to cybercrime and the elderly, check out this article by a gerontology nurse who explains in detail the overlapping risks facts that show up online for the elderly. https://www.healio.com/nursing/journals/jgn/2019-2-45-2/%7Bdeb3bffa-49dd-463c-b52a-501372c3698d%7D/cybercrime-a-new-and-growing-problem-for-older-adults

age also comes some general cognitive impairment as well, contributing to their vulnerability both online and even offline.

For both of these vulnerable groups, instincts pose the greatest threat to their own cybersecurity. For sure, we can tell each group, for example, to protect their passwords and not give them out, right? That is an easy rule to follow, unless you are a vulnerable senior who is socially engineered by someone online because their grandchild is traveling—and they know it—and without immediate assistance from Grandma or Grandpa, they are going to remain in jail, or be arrested, or be denied medical coverage, etc. Pick the evil used to exploit your elderly parent in that instance, but don't tell me they can't be easily moved to action by such a well-scripted personal plea. Or similarly, the scoundrels who prey on them with Social Security and Medicare scams, all destined to impose financial ruin, but which are so often enacted with such ease by skilled fraudsters abroad who will never be found and held accountable.

Teenagers are actually too savvy for most of that, and not likely sufficiently in the systems of government tracking and control to be as vulnerable to either identity theft or social engineering just quite yet. However, ALL teenagers are vulnerable to peer pressure and the social implications that being an outsider imposes on one's growing up experience. So, they seek affiliation and belonging—a powerful feeling of validation at a time of great vulnerability—and the crooks and cretins all know it. They are easy prey to luring, sexual exploitation and induced criminal behavior for the benefit of others. Signs start innocently at first but can quickly escalate. Again, this is a legitimate parental fear, but that is not a productive emotion that will help. We must be as proactive in replacing that fear with hope even as I admit these scams seem so prevalent as to be inescapable and are being talked about all the time stoking our fear.

Notably on that point, for each group, education and awareness alone are insufficient to trigger a positive change in behavior in the same way that base characteristics we explored in adults dictate to a large extent the way they behave on the job. Change is hard, and changing our personalities is even harder. So often we find ourselves acting out base instincts online rather than being mindful of the rules. This generates risk and can, ultimately, eliminate or reduce the rewards of being online and leave victims feeling stupid, ashamed, and disappointed in themselves for having fallen prey to an attack.

The solutions for each group seem superficially different; but, the similarities are worthy of examination because they can better assist us in protecting all the members of our extended family from online exploitation. An underlying assumption that is important here is that the risk of exploitation online—in so many ways—is an increasing not decreasing risk that the entire mechanism of the internet rises above national criminal laws making prosecutions and recoveries of those perpetrating cybercrime almost impossible internationally. As a result, the internet offers a quick, efficient, and very effective criminal platform on which to conduct schemes designed to harm us and so, once again, hypervigilance becomes a risk because it would simply seem almost impossible to help our seniors and young adults escape the risk of becoming a victim of online crime.

However, we know that this is not only unsustainable but unhealthy. And it will not ultimately keep these groups safer and may even deplete their enjoyment of being online. So, I take this opportunity to remind parents gently that denying access to the online world—even with good intentions or for their own protection—is an overwrought response that will not help either group in the end, and might even contribute to more anxiety, depression, self-loathing and fear. Careful navigation of the intersection point of individual psychology and these dangerous online waters is necessary, always with an eye to engaging these two most vulnerable groups among us to learn alongside us how to better empower themselves to become more cyberaware.

Let's begin this discussion with children: it is not helpful or appropriate to our children's mental health to focus on fear as a reason to behave in any particular way. Yet, we so frequently fall into this trap from an early age when we say things like: "look both ways before you cross the street." Obviously, this is sound advice because, if they don't do that, there is a real risk of injury or death if they are struck by a car. However, good parenting should focus on the payoff of safe outcomes from what should become natural, recurring behavior rather than on provoking this behavior from fear of consequences. While nuanced, and we may begin by using fear of negative consequences to provoke the auto-response, eventually, we have to get to a place with our children where this becomes simply what we do—automatic—and not as a response to a fear stimulus. When this is achieved, we have moved from hypervigilance to habit.

As it is so with cybersecurity: we need to gain for ourselves as adults sufficient understanding of the behaviors we seek to make habits in our children that will help make their online conduct safer. And while monitoring this for compliance early on may be appropriate as a starting point, we must get to the point where the habits are so ingrained, they occur without monitoring. They occur simply because they are associated with the activity itself: for instance, if I am online, I need to be aware of the need to validate at all times who I am engaged with and who they are in relationship to me. Are they known or unknown? What are the appropriate ways we act with those we can validate and know (our friends—online or otherwise) versus those that we do not, and what the implications are for crossing activity boundaries without doing so. Note my use of the word "implications" rather than "consequences" in a continuation of the theme of this book as moving away from fear-based compliance to a voluntary understanding of good and safe online habits for our children to learn and deploy.

And, just as we did for adults, we can use the concepts from the test if not the test itself, to help our children understand themselves and their own base instincts and inclinations as a way to help them develop safer online behaviors. Discuss openly with them your own experiences online and how you help yourself reduce fear and increase enjoyment of being online by remaining aware of the risk-reward trade-offs that you actively make. Help shape your children's understanding of cybersecurity within a context of enhancing opportunity and empowerment versus fear and anxiety. Over time, this will not only increase the likelihood of them being more compliant with good online practices, but it will also likely help them keep their own online behavior in check.

As parents, we also need to be mindful of a simple fact: as our children enter adolescence in particular, there is a natural separation that occurs between parent and child. As their bodies and minds drift toward independent adulthood and all that it fulsomely represents, this is a normal and natural occurrence. They will experiment more, take on aspects of identifying or considering their emerging values and choices from their own perspective instead of the parental viewpoint. This can be particularly excruciating in the context of online behavior where parents and other adults "in charge" worry about the permanency of the consequences from mistakes being made online. The result of this is often to contribute even more to our own sense of fear and dread about our children being online and we, in turn, become hypervigilant about their actions contributing to the fear present in both the parent and child.

As a society, we have yet to move in this direction fully, but we are going to need to learn to treat youthful online indiscretions as simply that: a mistake made at a point in time that, were it not for the permanent digital record, would not even be notable later in life or even likely known to most. This returns me to an important point from the Introduction, where the speed of technology change being driven by bit-tech is outstripping our collective social ability to evolve and adapt. Societies do not know what to do fast enough to keep up with the changes imposed on us by companies who care more about selling new technologies than they do about the social consequence of the technology itself. So, you have Google fighting hard to avoid the global adoption of the EU's "forget me" option where families and children can ensure that digital records of those youthful indiscretions do **not** become a life-long trail of self-destruction simply by remaining visible. There is no need for that. In every other element of our social systems (schools, justice system, healthcare and so on), we recognize that children and youth are not adults in temperament or consequence—and that sometimes an event is simply a teachable moment—rather than an indication of an irretrievable human failing. Why should internet search engines, for instance, be any different and why would Google fight this obvious benefit so vigorously? We simply need to catch up legal and social norms to technology, right?

They fight it because it is very expensive to maintain a system to collect, verify, and enact deletions to a technology that is like a data vacuum cleaner, never designed to add any judgment to the data it collects nor how it is displayed, only to collect it and display it according to algorithms of relevance known only to them. This is what makes Google both all-powerful and useful on one level—for the completeness of its ultimate search results—and also ignorant to the massive human consequence this can wreak if there is no way for anyone to keep something private and offline.

But lingering on this point, this phenomenon of *forever technical memory* does not simply plague kids. Any of us, me included, who may have incurred less than gracious or kind online coverage of important events at some point in time in our lives, understands what it's like to personally re-experience that over and over as it comes up time and time again. As a result of living online, it lives on longer than it would otherwise as something of a personal note.

This makes us afraid for our children and may coax us into fear-based conversations to try and help them avoid this same outcome for themselves because we fear it never being possible to fix. But that won't work, it may backfire, and, in the end, the real solution is for society, our laws, and our determination to hold Big Tech responsible entirely for managing the unintended consequences of their technology on individuals and that responsibility overrides any concern of ours for their profits.

If they build it, and we come, it must be on terms that are fair and socially balanced instead of tilted, unfairly, on some premise of them not being accountable for what is already published and propagated online. Nonsense. True or not, we all have privacy rights that should enable us to eliminate some kinds of content from being propagated online about us. Particularly in the United States, we do not take it as seriously as the EU does for instance[10]. Maybe we should, as consumers and parents, in terms of protecting ourselves online, determine it is high time that we agitated politically to support our children especially by ensuring that we all must recognize youthful indiscretions for what they are, and never let these formerly controlled and private events unfairly haunt children for a lifetime when that is not the standard we set and abide by in any other parts of our social or legal system. If Big Tech wants to build platforms that take advantage of our social systems, let them also bear the costs of supporting reparative mechanisms, such as requiring them to remove content when that's the right thing to do—making it simple and workable regardless of the cost—and holding them accountable in the design of their technologies that exploit our social nature to also never impair social development of our children and youth by not allowing these online mistakes to be fixed.

Our elderly and extended family, especially those that live alone or in more socially isolated circumstances, present a different challenge. It is unlikely that their behavior online will actually create some lingering electronic record that will impair their future—that is likely behind them and, particularly, most are likely retired from the world of work where this phenomenon, the permanent memory of the internet, is currently having the most negative impact on individuals unduly haunted by their past.

So, I suggest that the test referenced as a reader of this book is almost identical in impact to various state or provincial laws about driving tests for our seniors. It is never easy to have the conversation with our parents about considering giving up the keys to the car because it is no longer safe or appropriate for them to be driving themselves. Our parents see this as a deprivation of their independence, as us crossing the line as their children to inflicting unfair standards on them that are not our job to enforce, and it can antagonize an otherwise fine relationship to become the voice of reason that must impose this nec-

10   For more information on the progressive data protection and privacy provisions afforded to EU citizens now, please visit this official site for unbiased and original source information: https://eugdpr.org/

essary consequence. So, what do most of us do? We rely on the state to determine, through testing, whether or not our parents should still be driving.

Now, truth be told, many of us might be provoking that conversation either by age, through reporting or requesting or otherwise nudging a reluctant parent into the cognitive or physical driving test required to accomplish our objective of determining safe driving capability. But it is always easier to point to the test instead of our own judgment when implementing the consequence of the denial of a driving license.

Well...this cybersecurity profiling test can accomplish that same outcome when used in a similar way. It enables you to engage in conversations differently, by comparing test results for instance between parent and adult child, in order to help draw conclusions about the degree of safety that your parent is likely exhibiting online and how their instincts, born of personality traits, may be contributing to them being exploited and making them vulnerable. We reposition the conversation away from fear and toward opportunities to develop new awareness and habits that can help keep them safe while online. Note again the shift in language away from fear and consequences and toward the opportunity for control and responsibility for our actions that is embodied in this style of conversation, something my research demonstrates as a sensitization effect that the tool positively creates when used in this way. The test gives us language that makes vague concepts about cybersecurity and safety online more concrete and more accessible.

The almost playful comparisons that occur, the family banter about how much you are like your father/mother, etc. help reinforce the respect embedded in this conversation, arising from the application of the test, and turns it into a positive event designed to improve the online experience for your parent to make it more satisfying, safer, and less risky for them.

The result is a more immediate change in online behavior than is achieve by other methods, making our elderly family members feel empowered rather than disempowered or disconnected. That fulfills a significant social promise of this book to improve online safety.

This is the transformative effect that is so rewarding about this approach to cybersecurity generally: as we change the mood and tone of the conversation away from fear and toward hope, we increase the likelihood that individuals will receive this information in the helpful spirit from which it is offered. I am not suggesting that restricting or interdicting online access or choices is the answer. Rather, I propose ensuring that self-regulation of our own tendencies while online to avoid being exploited by others is best. This should not induce fear so much as active awareness and helps everyone in your family feel more secure, safer, and happier while online.

CHAPTER NINE:
BIG TECH ETHICS — FINAGLING, FAVORS, AND FINES

Throughout this book, you may detect a smug certainty that the ideals of capitalism are alive and well in American Big Tech companies who clearly exploit us for commercial gain. This is to be expected because the core tenets of capitalism suggest private sector firms maximize their self-interest unless bridled by law or regulation. And for all the current talk in US political circles about rampant socialism, there is no evidence to support this as any kind of threat to Big Tech profits in this country! In fact, to protect its powerful franchise, a close examination of Big Tech reveals mostly finagling, favors, and fines.

To begin, let's consider a relatively simple definition of socialism as "a political and economic theory of social organization which advocates that the means of production, distribution, and exchange should be owned or regulated by the community as a whole." This becomes ultimately ironic in the context of any social media platform, a major focus of consumer ire for the social plagues they continue to create while their creators all get rich at our expense.

If we were on the cusp of socialism sweeping America, it would be the *users* of Facebook, for example, that would represent the community in that definition and its users who should be getting rich. I can't speak for anyone else, but I don't remember getting my royalty, or loyalty, check for all the brilliant things I have posted on Facebook—did you?

If socialism is sweeping the country, how exactly are the means of production (binary code in 1s and 0s that essentially comprise the Facebook platform) and the collection and distribution of information provided **for free** by its users which are then **exchanged for advertising revenues** from others not benefitting us? I know this: most people are simply grateful Facebook is free—and they leave it at that. However, under a socialist model a mechanism would exist for you to share in the benefits of what you post and share. The more interesting your post that attracts view from others, the larger your share of Facebook's revenue would be. Akin to being a shareholder, we could create a new classification called "informationholder" where you are paid for giving up information about yourself, your activities, and preferences that would offer you profit sharing from their exploitation of you. How about that idea to dampen Big Tech's power and rebalance benefits of social media back to us? These kinds of ruminations are being called "new capitalism" by the media and others who believe that too much economic power and social influence are present in these massive tech firms[11].

Others (such as Shoshana Zuboff[12]) have delved into the business models of these tech titans to expose what she refers to as "surveillance capitalism", suggesting that while cloaking themselves in the greater economic good, tech firms are actually engaged in structural change for which the long view is not available, and exhibit power and control

---

11   While there are many examples to quote demonstrating the currency of this thinking, someone with whom many would not entirely agree but who is particularly clear about the problem is Barry Lynn and you can find an excellent summary of his position here: https://www.fastcompany.com/90416600/this-man-says-big-tech-is-the-greatest-threat-to-democracy-since-the-civil-war
12   https://www.foreignaffairs.com/reviews/review-essay/2019-10-10/new-masters-universe and similar

over tracks of our future economy that are akin to first-mover monopolies rather than legitimate competitive success.

Instead of engaging in these debates which are mostly threatening to them because they so often result in a clamor for more government regulation or to break up these firms, Big Tech likes to talk about the transformative effect of its products, promising it will all be good in the end. But how do we know this for a fact? This will only be proven retrospectively, if at all, and by then they will have reaped incredible profits, at our expense, while declining responsibility for the negative consequences their business models impose socially, morally, or politically right now. This seems unjust, and gives rise to core concerns about their business ethics.

Economists label these externalities: costs imposed on third parties not by choice by the production of goods or services when those real costs are not included in their production costs. What about the social damage wrought worldwide by these companies? Shouldn't we be measuring these negative impacts and charging at least some reparations for these damages back against their profits logically? Of course, we should, but we don't. And why not, you may ask.

Before answering that, reflect on the massive scale of those profits first. In its fiscal year 2018, Facebook publicly reported global revenues of ~$56 billion and net profits after expenses of ~ $25 billion representing a profit margin of 45%. These were up substantially from 2017, and their own forward forecasts suggest continuing upward trends into next year for number of subscribers and growing cross-platform revenues.

In addition, after paying all taxes (which it discloses as effectively a rate of only 13%—well below what one might expect and something else that should be of great concern to all of us and also the politicians who represent us), those results netted shareholders $7.57 in earnings per share on a fully diluted basis.[13] Furthermore, in a January 2019 call with stock market analysts, the company's CEO, COO, and CFO

13   https://s21.q4cdn.com/399680738/files/doc_financials/2018/Q4/Q4-2018-Earnings-Release.pdf

reported that 2018 was a "particularly difficult year" and not one which they hoped to repeat for a myriad of reasons very carefully document-ed by the *New York Times* and others.[14] Even more interesting is that Mark Zuckerberg, founder and still the current CEO, holds a con-trolling interest in the firm of 392 million shares representing almost 53% of the voting rights in the company. An examination of the share-holding of other tech titans such as Amazon, Google, Microsoft and the like would reveal similar dominant personal ownership of founds – a normal state in capitalism – but with an outsized proportion of the *total wealth* of the entire planet[15]. And the founder of Facebook is not even the wealthiest technology entrepreneur on the planet, Jeff Bezos the founder of Amazon is and by a healthy $3B dollars or so.

Essentially, Mr. Zuckerberg and his pals can pretty much do what they want with the companies they founded and still control, and per-haps this is the point. They did so under our existing system of capi-talism in a spectacularly successful way and should not be blamed for that. The incentives and mechanisms to achieve this kind of outsized wealth always existed historically (think railroad barons or maybe Henry Ford). But the dynamics of technology entrepreneurship are different, incorporating global incentives to misbehave commercially while benefitting personally founders who stand to reap potentially billions of dollars of sheer personal gain from financial performance of a company that is generating that wealth that is socially and politically irresponsible and not actually assuming liability for the consequences of its products.

Maybe I am alone in this thinking, though I doubt it. When Face-book reports these levels of profits, in supposedly dire times, why is it so resistant to investing those profits back into becoming a more

14   https://www.nytimes.com/2019/01/30/technology/facebook-earn-ings-revenue-profit.html

15   For facts that will make the average reader realize just how extreme this wealth gap is, consider these 11 facts about how wealthy the wealthiest tech founder really is: https://www.businessinsider.com/how-rich-is-jeff-bezos-mind-blowing-facts-net-worth-2019-4#2-bezos-makes-2489-per-second-more-than-twice-what-the-median-us-worker-makes-in-one-week-2

ethical and socially responsible company? There is obviously no lack of resources available to accomplish that goal. It would seem easy enough for them to make decisions to invest more heavily in content management systems, for instance, as the need to do so is obvious. And doing so would be a promise worth making and keeping I think. But even just recently, it announced under the guise of "protecting free speech" that it would not decline ads from politicians that it and everyone else knows to be false even as Twitter – competition for them – opted to do just the opposite and ban all political ads. Is Facebook just not then encouraging Russians and others to interfere yet again in our elections in 2020? Have we all learned nothing about that?[16] Let's recall that while he is busy defending this as "free speech" issue, which it most assuredly is not, while all these false paid political ads run, he profits personally and substantially from that decision. Yet another of big tech's bigger lies I think.

For such a sophisticated Big Tech company, always trying to convince us that their platform is safe for us to use; evidence is mounting it is not. Yet Facebook is not alone in the pursuit of activity that is not sustained by law or which transgresses regulations they were completely aware of but chose to ignore. For instance, just recently YouTube was fined for violations of COPPA—legislation designed to protect vulnerable children from online exploitation—and fined $170 million by the FTC[17]. Over several years, there are multiple examples, and types of significant data breaches or the breaking of laws occurring that perfectly prove my point about the *insecurity of cybersecurity* with so many of these tech giants, supposedly experts at what they do. Even they cannot keep themselves safe. And I wonder how many of those breaches may have had a human element to them as explored in this book? That would mean that Big Tech is as much at risk, if not more perhaps, than anyone else is from these kinds of cyberattacks, and they hold a treasure

---

16   https://www.vox.com/recode/2019/10/21/20925872/facebook-political-ads-russia-iran-zuckerberg-press-conference

17   https://www.nytimes.com/2019/09/06/technology/youtube-fine-child-privacy.html

trove of information about us the bad guys really want, too.

Also recently, the FTC confirmed it was imposing a history-making $5B fine[18]—noted by many as nothing short of a slap on the wrist for a company making this much money—for Facebook's breach of a previous privacy-protecting agreement with the FTC made eight years ago. This makes Facebook a confirmed recurring transgressor it seems.

This recent case arises from on-going exploitation of personal member data by third parties (in this case, Cambridge Analytica[19]) that users did not agree to and were unaware of. These do not suggest a company that takes its users' privacy seriously, does it? Or which operates ethically in the interests of its "community" rather than itself even?

It is also important to note that, by nature, the FTC's regulation of any industry is backward-looking. It must find past examples and pursue them in court, and its sole means of punishing the company is fines and agreements to eliminate any illegal practice it detected. In fact, as a feature of the Facebook settlement, the FTC even agreed that the $5 billion fine was sufficient to give Facebook a legal "release"—that is a do-over—so that *any past practice* it committed which violated privacy or consumer protection laws cannot be prosecuted now.

This finagling on Facebook's part was deliberate: does it know things we do not? Perhaps it was more knowingly engaging in some of these behaviors than it has publicly admitted and wanted this shield to protect itself from those transgressions it undertook.

And there is another problem the *Washington Post*, the *New York Times* and others have identified explicitly in their coverage of this story: since the restrictions on Facebook's data collection and processing only cover past malpractice (for example gathering phone numbers for

18   https://www.washingtonpost.com/opinions/a-5-billion-fine-wont-change-anything-at-facebook-and-theres-a-bigger-problem/2019/07/26/41ed411e-a73e-11e9-a3a6-ab670962db05_story.html?noredirect=on&utm_term=.cb555a1bf724
19   https://www.washingtonpost.com/opinions/a-5-billion-fine-wont-change-anything-at-facebook-and-theres-a-bigger-problem/2019/07/26/41ed411e-a73e-11e9-a3a6-ab670962db05_story.html?noredirect=on&utm_term=.cb555a1bf724

security and then repurposing them for advertising), this new agreement with the FTC contains no broader limits on using information gathered for one reason from being used for an altogether different purpose (for instance, combining data streams from across its various web platforms to coordinate the delivery of more targeted advertising to unsuspecting users).

Although there is some nominal documentation required now for any new product or service that Facebook delivers in the future, it is not really clear that self-disclosure and self-regulation of Facebook has worked in the past and I am dubious this effort will in the future.

This brings me around to this idea of favors: in 2018 there was a hue and cry in Washington, DC, about either breaking up or regulating Big Tech. While it is hard to imagine anything productive actually coming from Congress these days, even a growing chorus of this sort makes Big Tech nervous because they *know* what they're doing is wrong. Like kids with their hands in the information cookie jar, they want a few more bites before they get caught.

So, Congress demands Big Tech CEOs come before them to justify what they are going to do to improve online security for consumers as a result of the massive monopolies they hold[20]. I surmise Big Tech will yet again makes big promises and obfuscate about their true intentions, sucking unsuspecting politicians into conversations that make little sense and demonstrate no real understanding of the root problem. Of course, very few of the politicians were much better often having only a vague working knowledge of the technologies they claimed they wanted to now regulate. And I doubt in this current political climate, much will happen anyway.

While all this is not unusual, what is obvious is the extent to which politicians are somehow afraid of these Big Tech behemoths. Perhaps the answer lies, just as it does with big pharma and other self-interested companies that seek favors from Washington, in just how much

---

20   https://www.reuters.com/article/us-congress-tech-antitrust/big-tech-executives-due-on-capitol-hill-next-week-for-antitrust-hearing-idUSKCN1U42HF

they buy favors through political donations[21]. How can politicians who rely on these companies to fuel their campaigns hold them accountable through legislation? The irony of this runs deep, and it is not exclusive to Big Tech. But it is a factor in their freedom to operate without strong government regulation or scrutiny.

This returns to one of my earlier fundamental points: Facebook mostly fears one thing— to be truly held accountable for what it collects from posts on its system. Since inception, Facebook has relied on **not** being deemed a publisher, as defined at law, to shield itself from any corporate liability for what is posted on its platform. Yet, it takes no umbrage in exploiting all of this published personal content for its own gain, including the recent disclosure that internal efforts had identified over 100 million fake accounts likely linked to various foreign governments, agencies, and entities trying to gain influence in domestic politics to affect US elections. How ethical is it for Facebook to knowingly engage in a business model that is so easily exploited for nefarious purposes while shielding itself from responsibility for it? Meanwhile, fat cat politicians ignore this core problem, refuting adequate regulation.

I can tell you why: information friction or restrictions in its business model do not protect Facebook's profits. They will vigorously deflect anything that prevents it from accepting, propagating, and placing ads—even indiscriminately—all over its site directly tied to mining and exploiting insights from user information it collects unless ordered to do so[22]. Why would it, when its business model and adware platform make it billions of dollars? Incentives to maintain the status quo are intense, and billions of dollars of profit hang in the balance.

So, it spends piles of money to avoid disruption of any of that, including seeking favors or paying large fines when it misbehaves instead. It wants anyone to be able to easily sign up, start using Facebook,

---

21   https://www.opensecrets.org/orgs/totals.php?id=D000033563&cycle=2016

22   For intriguing recent developments concerning the integrity of adware platforms, learn more about the "Sleeping Giants" online campaign against Breitbart news for example. Maybe we are all waking up.

and share deeply personal information freely to grow their global reach to keep profits flowing. Impediments like assuring one's identity, detecting and preventing fraudulent accounts from its midst, or being responsible for the conduct of its subscribers are simply inconvenient and costly at the scope and scale that Facebook operates without massive investments in labor and systems development. That would be a sweeping overhaul of the platform and its founding premise of open, uncensored (and therefore non-libelous) posts.

To be fair to Big Tech, and specifically Facebook, some recent efforts are now visibly underway to redress some of these self-serving positions. Reportedly, they are now making investments that it ought to have willingly made previously knowing full well the danger its platform represents as a source of information exploitation, particularly through false accounts.

It is also clear that the chorus of voices demanding that Big Tech be more accountable are taking hold inside management of these companies. Proof of progress on this point includes the fact these recently launched efforts include some limited content management efforts. This finally suggests some limited acceptance by these companies of taking responsibility for what is posted on their systems, even if they are squeamish about possible charges of engaging in censorship, returning us to this very American definition of complete free speech. Maybe that is simply not possible on these platforms without incurring huge social risk.

Regardless of the presence of this valid concern about where such content management efforts start and stop, and what constitutes the boundaries of acceptable censorship, it should not have taken Facebook this long to arrive at this point. Ethically, their executive team has known for years the risks its platforms represented. It should have been investing heavily long before this in addressing that problem if we are to genuinely accept their claim that it takes ethics more seriously than it does economics. And they are hardly the only example of this.

The ethical imbalance of being unwilling to invest abundant profits in doing the right thing is proof that the capitalist system is alive and well in Silicon Valley. So, for the foreseeable future, socialism does not seem to be much of a threat to the staggering profits of Big Tech.

This recurring posture of reluctant action by Big Tech may explain the cacophony of political voices in Washington raising the siren song of "breaking up" Big Tech. This is an intriguing, if impractical, reaction[23]. As with so many companies that dominate key global industries—such as banking for example—what really is too big to fail? Or at what point does a company become so big that it is anti-competitive by definition?

This is not a trite question. Nor do I profess to know any specific answer to it. The United States is a firmly capitalist country with a powerful economic engine. This demands caution to not confuse commercial success or dominant market position with illegal monopolistic anti-competitive behavior. That is the only legal basis for any forced government move to corporately restructure Facebook or any company. Realistically nothing resembling evidence of Facebook being anything but an excellent competitor who had first-mover advantage as its starting point has been produced. Their size is a result of being a smart company that did well. That fact, and the abundant availability of smart venture capital, allowed it to grow and dominate its market. This is not a crime nor something that justifies government intervention.

But on the question of regulation, I take quite a different stance. The Founding Fathers who wrote the Constitution could never have anticipated a technology that would allow us to be attacked from within by foreign adversaries who never step foot on American soil. But that is exactly what social media platforms that stretch the globe really do. They facilitate actions from afar that have impact locally. However, because they are supra-national and hover above national laws often, we have no opportunity to easily apply laws or regulation—even if there is proof of criminal behavior online. This renders the global internet absolutely lawless in many respects. It is a technology Wild West of sorts.

23   https://fortune.com/2019/07/16/amazon-google-apple-facebook-hearing-senate/

This speaks to a growing need for coordinated government action among nations to regulate the internet and its activities globally. They need to struggle with how best to accomplish that, but regulation is needed that acknowledges both the global benefits but also the possible harms that are inherent in Big Tech business models. Our laws existed in the days when publishers and journalists all understood their particular codes and responsibilities of their conduct, and it had consequences. Using libel and slander law, you could hold publishers and the media accountable for stating mistruths and expect a printed retraction, for example.

Now, anybody can become an instant publisher or a news source without those same restrictions, codes of conduct, or legal standards. They can put out there online whatever they want to. It need not be factual, accurate, or even interesting to make it into print. That is a changed world economically and legally. This naturally demands a shift in our thinking about how to uphold accountability for online behavior, perhaps in ways more attuned to how the internet and its various social media platforms really work.

This book is not intended to diagnose and present those alternatives—I leave that to those more skilled in the legal arts and informed on policy minutia of global treaties. But to retain the long-term economic and social benefits of the internet intact, governments around the world need to work together to reduce online criminal potential. They need to step up enforcement in reply. The internet cannot remain lawless and unregulated because the majority of innocents online will eventually lose trust. That bigger economic implication should be reason enough for countries to band together and cooperate in enforcement to apply swift consequences for online crime.

But if not, or perhaps in companion to that suggestion, a key legal change that may offer us all potentially a silver bullet for social media misuse today is to simply declare Facebook and all similar platforms to be publishers, as defined at law. Although this would require dramatic changes in their platform and business model, it would mean joint accountability between author and publisher for anything that made it into print in the public realm. It's a game-changer by forcing Facebook and a host of other similar Big Tech giants like YouTube, Instagram, and others to be legally accountable for what is posted and distributed on their sites.

To make this easier to accomplish in practice, it would suggest a significant change in their business model from the free flow of information (open systems) to restricted or constricted information flows (closed systems). To avoid legal consequences as a publisher, this could include warning messages about certain types of content, for example. Or making some content age-restricted—which by definition now means securing proof of the validity of an account's ownership, the age of the owner and other legal certainties that would make Facebook shudder today. Or they could make their system operate such that only those who choose to follow you can see what you post, and that they would still have a way to report offensive or harmful content to an administrator for further action. Or they could impose restrictions on re-posting or sharing of content to make the broad impact of false information harder to accomplish.

All of these kinds of shifts in the regulatory burden from innocent users back onto corporate profiteer would ensure a very different kind of attention from Facebook and others when dealing with false, slanderous, or criminal content I can assure you. Because now they would be directly and corporately responsible for these impacts. And I guarantee more investments in much tighter content management would immediately follow such action.

So, what have we concluded in this chapter? That there is a rising and legitimate tide of concern politically around the country about regulating Big Tech in newly appropriate ways. There is a desire to force self-governance over new and very profitable business models that, while certainly contributing to the greater good, are also enablers for the greater bad. And that there are sufficient profits made by these companies and available to invest in new resources to accomplish all that. But all that requires Big Tech to voluntarily rebalance economic gain to improve ethical practice, something of which there is currently scant evidence. The likelihood of this happening without government intervention seems infinitesimal.

What is the logical next step available to you as consumers of online services? Uniting users to form a real sense of community, with its own intentions and aspirations to have input into how business is conducted around and with you is an excellent first step. Think of this as equivalent to unionizing when workers feel abused by management. In this case, the mere threat of users closing down and abandoning their Facebook accounts last year certainly got more immediate attention from their management team than did any whining in Washington, DC, about the commercial power or overreach of Big Tech. That is proof this method can work.

And this is simple to understand too: politicians take their cues from the electorate and, if we're serious, the entire Facebook business model is actually under our control if we want it to be. Why? Because they operate at the behest, even mercy, of tolerant users willing to engage and post regularly. When we've had enough, all we need to do is stop posting and sharing. Until there is tangible evidence of users' willingness to punish Big Tech by abandoning their participation unless issues of concern to them are addressed, nothing will fundamentally change.

There are few incentives if you are Facebook, or any other Big Tech company, to change because of the underlying competition between economics and ethics. So long as that endures, users need to be aware of this tug and force those corporate choices to the front and center of our political debates, while protecting themselves from being put into harm's way in the meantime.

C H A P T E R   T E N :

THE GEOPOLITICS OF CYBERSECURITY

In the early days of the internet, a mere few decades ago, the biggest threat arose from miscreant teenagers in their parents' basement. These were the early hackers. Driven by a mix of leisure, technical curiosity, and often plain attention-seeking, their ambition was rarely criminal—juvenile in almost every sense. They hacked simply because they could!

Over time, these amateurs were surpassed by organized groups of hackers who proved far more effective: online crime gangs and global hacktivist networks emerged. This happened when amateur efforts demonstrated the ease with which this activity could be undertaken and, by organizing and scaling it, these new players began to reap the rewards of mega-hacks—on the scale seen in the Equifax case for example, to which we have referred several times already. Cyberattacks became more common as they continued to be more lucrative for criminal hackers. Later, in a predictable ramping up cycle, we then saw the entry of state-sponsored groups undertaking these hacks and attacks. In fact, these hacks/attacks have now become relentless.

A good example is North Korea. Initially, it built cyber capability to restrict citizen access to the outside world. This reinforced the ruling family's continuing cult of personality built around three generations of sustained dictatorship. Their latest egomaniacal leader, Kim Jong-un—Dear Respected—sees anything that challenges his leadership as a threat to be eradicated, even when the apparent threat is more ego-injuring than leadership-busting in nature.

When Sony Pictures released the movie, *The Interview*, a comedy poking considerable fun at North Korea's dictator and wounded his ego, he instructed his country's cybersecurity resources to hack the company and, apparently, offered individual hackers financial incentives to do so. And off to work they went.

On November 24, 2014, a group identifying itself as the Guardians of Peace—since directly attributed to North Korea's government—successfully hacked and then released confidential information very embarrassing to the company, including e-mails among employees criticizing Hollywood talent, executive salary and bonus information, new project plans, etc. This marked a shift in cybersecurity objectives: the information that was released had limited or no commercial value but was particularly about shaming the company for its actions. It was payback for what North Korea saw as a transgression against its culture and country.

Now imagine that you are Sony, a private company, and your adversary is an isolated dictatorship worlds away but with comparably unlimited cybersecurity resources and skills and all they want is to hurt your brand in retaliation for an apparent slight. That is not a crime with a financial incentive, but with a geopolitical motive. That's different. And increasingly, we see this kind of spurious attack, less rational but still criminal in intent, but provoked because your company happened to wound a bully dictator's ego online for example. This poses another dimension of risk for many organizations: What do you do when previously simple business decisions now carry online geopolitical risk? Again, I bring this fact to your attention not as an attempt to induce yet more fear; but to acquire knowledge that is empowering and which can help us all better understand the online motivations of others.

So, continuing the narrative, once North Korea realized how good its relative cybersecurity skills actually were, the rewards for successfully conducting cybercrimes increased. The regime began redeploying their significant national cybersecurity assets from conducting political surveillance, censorship, and shaming attacks toward theft campaigns that were more the domain of cybercrime gangs in Eastern Europe. They found the results were quite rewarding for such a poor country, and used this to raise funds around UN-imposed economic sanctions.

As a result, North Korean state-employed hackers have now been implicated in cyberattacks against banking systems in places like Bangladesh, Vietnam, Ecuador, and Poland, stealing at least $95 million (US) to date. These are big-time online bank robberies with an objective to raise much-needed cash to reduce the impact of US sanctions on their economy. Immediately we see a new geopolitical intersection where appropriate diplomatic efforts to force a dictatorship to behave better become triggers that increase cybercrimes targeting private interests. Geopolitics and the internet have now intersected with agonizing impact.

This suggests that a more sophisticated approach to online risk management and cybersecurity is vital, particularly in global organizations with international operations, because the threat assessment calculus is not just technical, but geopolitical in nature. What might the actions of one government do to contribute to putting a private company in harm's way elsewhere even if unintentionally? Or does a company's business with government provoke unknown or unpredictable cybersecurity risks? With whom is it safe to do business with anymore with all of these intersecting geopolitical interests converging all at once?

A further example of this complicated geopolitical calculus can be found in the Chinese ICT firm Huawei. Many readers are likely aware to some degree of this story from all the media coverage. This privately-owned, Chinese company is a successful and now dominant manufacturer of telecommunications switching equipment for telephone companies. It also produces consumer electronics, particularly cell phones. Based on global market share, it is respectively #1 and #2 in these two critically important industries. It has divisions around the world and is truly multinational, employing people from many countries across its operations.

Of course, China is a country that openly both controls its economy and assumes that Chinese companies, even private ones, will cooperate with the government on demand. This fact is enshrined in national law. Like North Korea, they also engage in extensive government-sponsored efforts to control its citizen access to the free web and in censorship of anything critical of the Chinese communist party or its way of governing. They are also the #1 perpetrator of international online theft of intellectual property—patents, trade secrets, and information that can help Chinese industry become more competitive against us—as part of its Made in China 2025 Plan, details of which are not at all secret and easily available online[24].

This kind of organized criminal activity is abhorrent to contemplate if you are American. Can you imagine our government actively seeking to encourage companies to steal trade secrets for our national benefit? But China intends to continue its ascent to global superpower status, and online IP theft is just a part of achieving this goal for them. This creates a competitive imbalance that Trump's trade war with China is partially intended to address: how can we eliminate state-sponsored incentives toward conducting online theft against US companies, so we don't have to level the playing field by reducing ourselves to that same game? Instead of stooping to steal secrets from China in response, the US hopes for a legal reversal that would see China recognize the value of properly developing and protecting commercial IP instead. While that may or may not be achieved, at least there is finally recognition and discussion of this vast problem in open global forums where debate can help produce solutions to this dilemma.

But let's return to Huawei. Well beyond theft, the US government has a much larger issue at stake. As Huawei became more competitive

24   https://en.wikipedia.org/wiki/Made_in_China_2025

and offered 5G cellular network equipment at costs that US and European companies could not match, this supplier's equipment became the backbone of the global internet in many countries including the US. Suddenly, the US government was faced with a situation whereby a Chinese manufacturer—with a legal duty to support the Chinese government as instructed—likely had a backdoor ability to monitor cellular communications of any country at any time on command. Now take that to a worst-case scenario, and we find ourselves at cyberwar with China where Huawei made equipment becomes an asset or even a weapon for the Chinese, perhaps with a hidden capability of shutting down US cellular networks or preventing cyber counterattacks for example. These are the flavor of really important geopolitical questions now in play across all superpowers globally.

One can easily see how the dynamics of global e-commerce, differing politics, and where technology is invented and manufactured intersecting in now interrelated domains where actions and reactions of both private companies and national governments have interesting and overlapping consequences. And all of this can have personal consequences for you too.

Canada, my original home and native land, is a peaceful and well-liked country generally. Yet it found itself wounded in the cross fire of this new geopolitical intersection. On demand from the US, and under a long-standing and legal extradition treaty, it arrested Meng Wanzhou[25]—the daughter of the company's founder and also its CFO—in transit through Vancouver which she often did to avoid being on US soil. This was legal because the US had previously charged Huawei and Meng herself with bank and wire fraud in regard to accusations that its US subsidiary had violated tough American sanctions against Iran. This really put Canada in a difficult legal and diplomatic spot.

The tense situation pitted two allies—the US and Canada with long-standing legal co-operation agreements and a history of being close allies—against China, who as a superpower itself, saw this as a

---

25   https://www.reuters.com/article/us-usa-china-huawei-tech/huawei-cfo-suing-canada-over-december-arrest-idUSKCN1QK0RW

national transgression of its independence as a nation when a prominent Chinese citizen was taken into custody on the basis of a US international policy with which it did not agree and which it saw as being against its own national and economic interests. This is a really great example of a complicated geopolitical dilemma of some note for all concerned.

Not only has this initiated multiple lawsuits of various kinds and significant diplomatic detritus and posturing too, but eventually the Chinese government retaliated by arresting two Canadians living in China on what many see as—forgive the pun—trumped-up charges.

The arrested individuals had absolutely nothing to do with Huawei or the issues at hand. They are innocent victims who happened to be in the wrong place at the wrong time, a classic personal risk scenario. But the origins of putting them in harm's way arise from an issue related to technology progress yet again. Let's remember this was done on behalf of supposed harm done to a company that claims independence from the Chinese government in its own marketing. But how independent is the company really that, when its personal owners are properly arrested, the state intervenes to arrest and hold innocent civilians in retaliation?

Perhaps the US had it right all along, and this firm is not quite as independent from the Chinese government as it purports to be. That question remains open and unaddressed in fact rather than simply by edict of statements made by both Huawei and the Chinese government.

While this single situation is still on-going, it is another intriguing example of the crossover between global politics, Big Tech, and the emergent battle for national domination of our interconnected digital world. We can remain naïve to all this and is all the more reason for individuals to be more aware of and engaged in these important global issues. While perhaps precedent-setting in minor respects, it is not likely to be the last of sticky situations like this.

A shift of focus on the internet itself also contributes to the rising stakes of global cybersecurity in new ways. This growing network of networks is evolving from communications between systems operated by humans, to autonomous systems running themselves in an increasingly digital world. This is tied to the concept of the Fourth Industrial Revolution involving robots, artificial systems, and autonomous systems that are quickly impacting all of us.

While the reported statistics vary globally, most estimates suggest about nine billion "things" are already online globally and interconnected, giving birth to "the internet of things" (IoT). In the next decade as this trend accelerates, that number of devices will at least triple. But more relevant to our discussion is that most of these new devices will shift from being computers, tablets, or smartphones to new objects like self-driving cars, smart thermostats, video doorbells, remote cameras and monitors, security systems, household appliances, and the like.

This massive expansion won't just grow the internet economy and benefit existing and new Big Tech players. It will also contribute to a growing attack surface, creating millions of new potential points of vulnerability where cyber threats originate. But that is not what they are marketing to us as consumers. Instead, we are sold on the convenience these innovations will offer us, not the threats it creates.

And with almost no regulation in place to force even basic legal liability onto the vendors of these new devices, most consumers will remain blissfully unaware of the growing danger these devices pose to them. They will make the global cybersecurity problem far worse. But it could also be that it results in the rise of such a nuisance factor that these continuing attacks lead to a hue and cry from users for better cybersecurity solutions from vendors that we enjoy today.

As wide-ranging as all the previous political, economic, and technical risks are in scope and scale, the more disturbing trend in global cybersecurity is that this is no longer just hacking systems. *Rather, it is about hacking human minds and disrupting adversaries' social and political systems.* This renders true global cybersecurity as a mostly non-technical challenge, more akin to a complex geopolitical game of online chess involving worldwide political cause and effect instead of simpler questions of national network security.

From the beginning, there was early evidence that the internet—and its associated technologies—were transformative. And they absolutely are. But the addition of global social media platforms on top of the worldwide web has severely reinforced that effect, perhaps making the primary issue negative social transformations technology now evokes. This means struggling not so much with the pace of technology change, but the speed of social adaptation it demands. This makes the psychology and sociology impact of the internet, both personally and professionally more important to master for us than any underlying technical architectures.

In that realm, one also imagines existing superpowers and the citizens of countries like the US, Russia, and China all now wondering what they could and should do to harness that transformative power for national gain, just as they do with any other technology advance that has occurred historically. Similarly, other well-developed countries, particularly those with a strong, technically-capable military such as the UK, Israel, and Germany began embedding digital capability—cyberweapons if you will—into their arsenals to match the technical capability of the cyber superpowers. This has created a type of cyber arms race that blends cyber deterrence and defensive actions to protect one's country and populace as they move online with offensive cyber war which is used to either actually or theoretically create a situation of online détente where actions taken against one country are likely met with cyber counterattack to keep things in check.

Now blend into this already complicated geopolitical mix, the actions of bad state actors who are often quite unpredictable (such as North Korea and Iran for instance) and you have a powder keg of influence, intrigue, and online activity all being undertaken to assert control over something which, by definition, rises above each individual state or nation. It actually reaches across and through them instead. Diplomatically and legally complicated indeed!

It is into this geopolitical mess that this chapter journeys as we try and contextualize cybersecurity as a global geopolitical issue that, ironically, also emanates from the personalities and cultures of the humans who are leading our nations, linking into the book's overall theme of exploring the human side of cybersecurity through the lens of personality.

I note this profound shift also deeply affects the cybersecurity profession, which must rapidly move into a fundamentally different place of emphasis. While none of the legacy technical issues that defined the early days of online cybersecurity efforts have receded, these have been displaced in importance by the emergence of the thornier geopolitical and societal challenges noted above. If the United States and its Western allies want to have an effective cybersecurity strategy, this new global threat environment must be assessed and understood, and collective and determined action taken that rises above any one particular nation's self-interest. Just as it is for the collective cybersecurity of a single organization, it is teamwork and the strengthening of alliances across common online interests that will more effectively combat inherently complex geopolitics.

Historically, a cornerstone of US cybersecurity policy has been a primary reliance on cyber deterrence. This has been enacted by combining national cyber capabilities (particularly intelligence apparatus and military strength through the US Cyber Command) while gaining influence over global norms that are intended to guide and control the range of online behavior nations are prepared to tolerate. These efforts date back to the emergence of the internet itself and the early identification that it challenged existing national legal norms to the breaking point.

Here is an interesting side note: the first trigger for deeper government awareness of the impact of the internet and its need to act was, of course, issues of online taxation. As soon as the implications for how money and wealth were being moved online became obvious, government was interested! At this point, when any new technology impacts something as central to a nation as its tax regime, it is amazing how quickly that new threat gets government attention. So, with the growing awareness of just how much we needed to re-think things with the rise of e-commerce, the US set about trying to gain advantage globally for regulating and controlling the internet.

Today we are in a period where this strategy may be deemed a failure. Or is at least on the cusp of collapse. For years, Russia has conducted successful attacks on the American political system, as well as on our various Western allies, with no substantive consequence. While these attacks started years ago, they peaked during the 2016 election and continue to the present as recently concluded by the Mueller Report and now obviously engaging the 2020 election once again. We must not be naïve about the objective of these attacks either as they are not of trivial consequence, creating political strife and social division among us.

The targets include not only the obviously expected ones (such as the Democratic or Republican National Committees or hacking various branches of the government for instance), but also general efforts to target Americans personally and domestically by sowing and stoking fear, division, and racial hate among us. Of course, the ultimate intention of these is not just to influence elections, but rather to destabilize our democracy and undermine our place in the world. And what have they learned through doing this? That some among us are more susceptible to disinformation and manipulation than others, feeding right into the overall hypothesis of this book about our collective need to be reflective about this point.

Denial—or worse, letting this issue be politically weaponized—actually helps the Russians achieve their goal of dividing us internally to eliminate collective action on our part that could keep our nation safer externally. If we are twisted up internally, we are a less effective global superpower. We must not let these attacks continue lest Russia prevail.

We must also be mindful, as thoughtful citizens of a leading democracy, that this is not just about political targets, but also the evolution of tactics and learning about what works when our enemy has an opportunity to pilot new methods of spreading disinformation among us. That fact alone threatens the functioning of an effective democracy.

The seizure of the Crimean Peninsula also gave Russia another strategic advantage that was, perhaps, even more valuable than port access to the Black Sea. Since before it even pretexted its invasion as an effort to support a suppressed Russian minority in the Ukraine, Russia was using its pending military action against Ukraine to test a variety of cyber weapons, disinformation tools, and campaigns for their effectiveness. It was a kind of battle lab for a whole range of new cyber threats and tactics. This helped them learn ways to evade detection of these methods and figure out what they could get away with and what would and would not work well. That is valuable insight in the emerging landscape of offensive cyberwar and active disinformation campaigns.

In addition, they further launched new cyber weapons that targeted civilian impact including power grids, nuclear power plants, water dams, and other nightmare cyberattacks on domestic infrastructure that, if successfully deployed, would have truly devastating consequences. And ultimately, all this was accomplished with nothing more than a diplomatic slap on the wrist. It is mystifying how silent the US government has been on this point.

Again, we see something intriguing to reflect on about these developments: these attacks are *not* just about stealing citizens' private information anymore. That is yesterday's news. We face a new plague of enemies using our own systems to reach straight into the homeland, mostly posing as legitimate users but with nefarious intent. This manipulation is different than outright attacks on the integrity of Big Tech's data security and cybersecurity efforts because it does not require any breach or hack to take place. They walk in the front door and simply use the systems that Big Tech has made available to all of us while denying any responsibility to fix that.

How can Big Tech make claims to keep us safe even as they profit from falsely established profiles which buy ads, share data, or interact just like all other users and which, to date, the social media platforms particularly have not really found effective ways to quickly detect and stop? In what other industry would we permit a product to be developed and sold that was inherently dangerous to its users and not hold the company accountable? I cannot think of any. This again invokes the concept of social externalities—those costs and impacts not accounted for in Big Tech's revenues and costs—but which are damaging to all the rest of us.

These terrible social developments, with no firm government resolve to redress or any meaningful solutions derived by Big Tech itself, have essentially produced a reduction in cybersecurity globally by allowing the world's cyberbullies to prevail and operate unhindered.

More ominously, these trends might actually create the opposite of deterrence by creating incentives for the superpowers to try and dominate each other in cyberspace. Then what? Our failure to clearly respond has taught not just Russia—a notable global bully—but many of our other enemies who see that undermining other nations is all gain and no pain, virtually speaking. Until this dynamic changes, we should expect to see not just Russia participate in these efforts, but also many other nations and non-state actors looking to achieve similar gains.

Key to our understanding of geopolitical cybersecurity then is that *the hacking of digital systems is quickly taking a back seat to larger efforts to hack human minds*, a much more dangerous, but potentially remunerative, undertaking. Our best line of defense against this rests with each of us individually and our ability to suspect and detect when we are being personally hacked, returning me to the whole point of my test. This effectively means that social media has been weaponized and is being used as a tool to accomplish human hacking, something that we should not accept and cower in fear of, but replace with a determined effort to prevent.

There is no better proof of the dangerous scale of this fact than the 2016 US election during which, on Facebook alone, 126 million Americans saw ads and posts from Russian trolls exploiting false identities to pose as political activists. Similarly, in just the last ten weeks of the campaign, fake accounts now known to be under direct Russian control, but posing as Americans, generated 2.12 million election-related tweets, receiving 454.7 million impressions within their first seven days of posting. That is staggering reach and impact, and I fear one that will likely be repeated in this coming election cycle too.

Unfortunately I must conclude that obvious denial at the top in both the US government and Big Tech leave me aghast. I wonder how the world will ever come to grips with this expanding geopolitical threat, a massive cybersecurity challenge that involves human rather than technical hacking. These developments lay waste to disingenuous claims of Big Tech about the rosy future of a technology-driven and socially interconnected world—because technology is now creating many more problems than it solves today.

Unless Big Tech accepts responsibility for the harm their systems pose, and implement solutions they develop, deploy, and pay for to mitigate them, their triumphant claims of progress ring hollow and should be seen as being as meaningless as they truly are.

01101001100011010101

CONCLUSION:
GROWING ONLINE HOPE

Fear is a dangerous contagion that drives bad behavior. That is really a summary of the whole point of this book. We also know fear induces harm in the human body, and I think our minds and souls too. Increasingly, technology is driving new fears into us as we are constantly reminded about its potential to harm us, even while we enjoy the benefits it can offer

While Big Tech touts all the good that it can offer, it is often in denial about the harm it inflict. This double-edged sword is cutting deep as the world careens toward being evermore globally interconnected online and cybersecurity breaches become a global plague. Instead, we must seek to find ways to be more hopeful about our global online future and to ensure that we work together as a society to harness good from technology innovation.

As our fear grows, humans move individually and collectively into a state of hyperarousal and/or hypervigilance that is autonomic and beyond our control. In some, this is more obvious and disruptive; and in others more subtle, even subconscious. But being in this state is hard on us. And it's *exhausting*. Given that is unsustainable, we need an alternative.

If we constantly worry about where the next online trap is going to ensnare us or our family members or co-workers, wreaking havoc with our credit, identity, or personal information, this will not stop. In turn, solution providers know the power of stoking fear in their marketing, and exploit our natural human desire to escape this stress. While they market a variety of tools that are supposed to make us safer, many of these solutions don't or only marginally help. My proposition is different: consumers can and should do somethings to keep themselves safe online instead. I know from years of experience this helps reduce online fear.

Ultimately, taking any action will make us temporarily feel better by seeming to transfer this risk and fear to someone else. But the root of the real problem is being *at risk because of our own behavior*. We cannot outsource our cybersecurity to others. And once we experience being hacked even when we have taken all the recommended technology steps, the fear returns. This is because we are tackling the problem from the wrong perspective.

Big Tech makes us all a promise it cannot keep: our online safety is *not* a technology problem but a human problem. Strengthening their codes and systems to eliminate cybersecurity risks is not working, and will never keep us all safe. Rather, the challenge that Big Tech knows but doesn't admit is the really big problem with technology is that most of the potential harm it can cause devolves from human factors and motivations, not technical imperfections. To achieve long-term cybersecurity requires us all to change our behavior and become more cyberaware and that is actually the blueprint for moving from online fear to hope that this book offers.

The benefit of taking responsibility for ourselves online instead of relying on Big Tech's false promises, is that it alleviates fear and reduces our stress. And that is what I hope this book has helped you to accomplish: a sense of how to reduce your fear of technology and replace that with hope. I have made this my professional mission.

Of course, I am not naively assuming that the knowledge contained in this book is a panacea that will solve the world's cybersecurity problems. Far from it, because the problems are just too big and the scale too global. Some people will simply not access this knowledge or might even prefer to remain in a state of ignorance, even though it drives fear. Some people who come into contact with this new knowledge will be skeptical—perhaps even afraid of something as simple as taking the test—and will not be able to harvest its benefits as a result.

But as an author, I rely on the few, not the many, for whom this book will represent a breakthrough in their thinking they will deeply appreciate. This new knowledge can help them address their online behavior using insights derived from the test results and this book to inspire them to become accountable for their own cybersecurity destiny. This turn from reliance on others to self-reliance, at the outset, can temporarily increase fear and you should expect this. Can I really do this you may wonder? What if I fail or what if it doesn't work? But as you take constructive steps to grow your knowledge, increase your confidence, and become aware of how your own bad habits can be exploited against you, fear is reduced. You gain control finally, and are in a position to make informed choices about your own use of technology in your own way.

At this point, you are also Big Tech's worst nightmare: a truly informed consumer. One who is willing to challenge technology companies to be better and to ensure they also take responsibility for their fair share of this growing cybersecurity problem. Perhaps you become more politically active, demand that both sides in our divided country stop weaponizing information for their own benefit and instead turn their attention to legislating obvious solutions to hold Big Tech more accountable for the costly social externalities that its systems are creating. And maybe you'll stop using some systems, or in some ways, perhaps not reposting that false tweet or falling prey to that hoax site just one day at a time as you become more information literate and discerning about who is trying to leverage you from afar to your own detriment and to that of our civil society as a whole.

So that really is ultimately my intent—to help reduce our fear of technology by exposing the lies and broken promises Big Tech regularly makes. There is no hope that Big Tech can deliver on any promise to keep us safe online. And they know this. But now so do we.

Instead, we must act for ourselves under our own accord with accountability for our online actions. This replaces the false hope propagated by Big Tech with empowering and constructive self-reliance. Enhancing your understanding of your own inherent personality traits as they relate to cybersecurity helps you take effective individual action to keep yourself safe. As you accept this, the reward is that it reduces fear and improves the benefits of being online. Over time, as we all collectively do this, we may have hope that the promise of positive social impact of new technologies for our own good is true and can be realized if we take action for ourselves to harness that good. But to do so, we must stop falling prey to false promises proffered by Big Tech. Their overpowering marketing hype, promises of changing the world always for the better, and denying the externalities and risks their technology impose are self-serving. Big Tech lies and denies, caring more about their own economic gain than they do about legal, ethical and safe conduct online.

And that, friends, is ultimately my point: we must count on ourselves and <u>not</u> them. It is our responsibility to save ourselves from ourselves, and to make the future online world we have created and now inhabit a better place for us all!

MORE INFORMATION

To understand more about the test and its practical applications for you and your family, please visit

CYBERCONTHEBOOK.COM

For organization-wide programs or cybersecurity consulting based on our patent-pending methods, visit our corporate site at **cyberconIQ.com.** Here you will find cost-effective ways to implement the test and accompanying online training to immediately improve your company's overall cybersecurity risk profile and compliance.

If you would like to explore having Dr. Norrie do a keynote at your event or company, please visit **cyberconthebook.com/bookings/.**

For up-to-date information about cyberconIQ and the latest cyber security trends, please follow us on social media:

@cybercon.thebook

cybercon.thebook
or
cyberconiq

9 781734 221091